THÉRÈSE OF LISIEUX

A Vocation of Love

Originally published in French under the title of *Je Souleverai Le Monde* by Societe Saint-Paul, pour l'Apostolate des Editions, 1980

THÉRÈSE OF LISIEUX

A Vocation of Love

by Marie-Pascale Ducrocq

Translated by Robert Jollett, M.S.C.,
from the 2nd Edition

ALBA · HOUSE NEW · YORK

SOCIETY OF ST. PAUL, 2187 VICTORY BLVD., STATEN ISLAND, NEW YORK 10314

Library of Congress Cataloging in Publication Data

Ducrocq, Marie Pascale.
  Thérèse of Lisieux, a vocation of love.

  Translation of: Je soulèverai le monde.
I. Thérèse, de Lisieux, Saint, 1873-1897. 2. Christian
saints—France—Lisieux—Biography. 3. Lisieux (France)
—Biography. I. Title.
BX4700.T5D8313   282'.092'4 [B]   81-20512
ISBN 0-8189-0431-3   AACR2

Designed, printed and bound in the United States of
America by the Fathers and Brothers of the
Society of St. Paul, 2187 Victory Boulevard,
Staten Island, New York 10314, as part of their
communications apostolate.

1 2 3 4 5 6 7 8 9 (Current Printing: first digit).

Table of Contents

Preface

Something new on Thérèse of Lisieux? After all that has been written we can doubt it, yet there is! This little book does contain something new. It is distinctive of great writers ever to prompt a new message.

I Shall Lift up the World (the original French title) conjures in my mind that face brought back to us by a photograph well-known today. In a few days Thérèse Martin is to enter Carmel. She smiles at the life awaiting her, her wide-open eyes stare unflinchingly at all that lies ahead for her. At the same time her gaze reaches far beyond, responding to a call which, from the heart of the Church, already makes her live all the vocations she will imagine and opens before her horizons as vast as the world.

Is it hard to find behind these features that trustful love which will be the lever so sought for, which with God for its fulcrum, will enable Thérèse to lift up the world? The six words of the title state Thérèse of Lisieux' whole life.

What is to be sought for in these pages, which go much farther, is not a summary, but a leap forward.

Sister Marie-Pascale's book is not meant primarily to teach. It confronts us with questions concerning our own lives. It should be read with the conviction that we have something, something important, to do in the world such as it is being built today. We too are called to "lift up the world." We shall if we are able to support ourselves on God.

Let ourselves then be caught up in the vital movement animating these chapters, by the appeal to conversion they would have us hearken to, often borrowing the very words of Saint Thérèse, by the love—in all its dimensions, and the trust—in all its depths, which they would arouse in us: in God to go beyond one's self to lift up the world; or rather lift up the world by lifting up one's self. By inviting us to a renewed experiencing of charity and of trust, this book aims at attaining and transforming our lives' innermost and most decisive well-springs. No greater lesson could be taught us.

These pages were spiritual conferences before being assembled into book form. They are from a Dominican monastery I know well from having preached there often, from a cloistered nun who left for Africa three years ago to found a new monastery in Burundi. There the original notes reached their final draft.

Happy coincidence! A contemplative voice from Africa helping us rediscover Saint Thérèse of the Child Jesus exactly fifty years after the Church proclaimed her Patroness of the Missions.

I Shall Lift up the World. Yes, these words fully express Saint Thérèse's ardent soul. Its being so well set in relief by the author deserves our gratitude.

Fr. Vincent de Couesnongle, O.P.
Master General

The reference abbreviations to the works of Thérèse are from the critical edition of her complete works, known as the "Edition du Centenaire." Reproduced by permission from the publishers.

Ms A, B, C	Manuscrit A, B, C.
Lt	Lettres de Thérèse.
CJ	Carnet jaune (yellow notebook) de Mère Agnès.
CMG	Carnets manuscrits de Sr. Geneviève.
NV	Novissima Verba (last words).

Conseils et souvenirs (counsels and reminiscences): Foi vivante, Cerf, 1973.

Introduction

All friends of Saint Thérèse of the Child Jesus know very well nothing can beat reading directly out of her own writings, but no doubt they also understand that anyone who has read much of her and prayed her much needs eventually to talk about her. After so many excellent books and articles have searched Thérèse's life and doctrine, analyzed, commented and avidly pressed them on every side, the only need is to simplify the whole. Now that she has over a hundred years of accumulated history around her, who knows whether in her eternity the little Carmelite might not wish to see everything reduced to the essential. We are fully aware that only God knows her true features, and she in Him. She will disclose them to us when we meet in paradise, and then perhaps we shall see more clearly how they were already here on earth wonderfully attuned to God's simplicity.

It has been said she was the revealer of Hope, the saint of abandonment, a perfect model of humility, the master of spiritual childliness. A great big book, still pertinent, disclosed and described running through her whole life a "dynamics of trust." Another, unpublished, would have spring from her smallness-mercy intuition a whole doctrine on predestination. Then we have too the charm of her simplicity, her sense of the Gospel, of the Church, her mission-mindedness, her discoveries regarding brotherly love, etc. This inventory of Thérèse's wealth, so abundant and so true, should not make us forget that she is first of all the saint of love, and of the love of God first of all.

That she is the saint of love everyone knows. Thérèse herself has stated so as clearly as possible:

"My vocation is love." (Ms B, folio 3)

A few weeks before she died, her one desire: "To love, to be loved, and to come back on earth." (CMG, July, 1897)

She defined her mission unequivocally: "I feel above all that my mission is about to commence, my mission of making God loved as I love Him . . ." (CJ, July 17)

In the same period, very shortly before her death, the desires dearest to her heart are expressed in a short prayer which she would have Abbé Bellière say for her each day: "Merciful Father, in the name of Your dear Son Jesus, of the Virgin Mary and of the saints, I ask you to inflame Sister with Your Spirit of love, and to grant her the grace of making You greatly loved." (LT, Feb. 24, 1897)

Finally, the very last words she muttered, "Oh,

I love Him . . . My God . . . I . . . love You." (CJ, Sept. 30)

In a way, it is not surprising that a whole variety of enlightening reflections were later drawn from Thérèse's written or oral recollections, reflections which she of course had not all explicitly stated but which she had definitely forefelt and even wanted when, choosing "everything," she had exclaimed, "I understood that love contained all vocations!" (Ms B, folio 3) This indeed explains the seminal power of Thérèse's message: Love is infinite, so by a stroke of genius inspired by Love itself, she took her stand in the center. Here all saints meet, but she had the grace to give it a unique expression. Limited in her lifetime by her era, her cloister, her age and her style, she managed from above to break free: "I cannot reflect a great deal on the happiness awaiting me in heaven; one expectation makes my heart beat, the love I shall receive and the love I shall be able to give." (CJ, July 13)

We perhaps no longer always look at the saint's works and above all her life in this surging of Love. Thérèse, like everyone else, was marked by her family background, by her health, her sisters, her temper, her bursting enthusiasm and her moody spells, but throughout all this, she gave herself up completely to Love, and never regretted it: "I am not sorry I gave myself up for Love . . . Oh, no I don't. On the contrary!" (CJ, Sept. 30)

May she herself help us always "to come back towards the true, dear light of love." (Ms A, folio 38)

It takes Father François de Sainte-Marie's table of quotations to realize how little space is given in her Manuscripts to certain words of Thérèsian vocabulary which supplied tons of books and articles:

Abandonment (*abandon*): only twelve quotations, although these are important ones.

Trust (*confiance*): fifteen quotations.

Hope: twenty-two, only a few concerning theological hope.

Way (*voie*): about the same. The famous little way (*petite voie*) Thérèse mentions specifically only once!

But *love* and *to love* count by whole columns, as though Thérèse had but this word in her mouth:

Approximately six columns for the word "to love" (*aimer*).

Six and a half for love (*amour*).

Six for heart.

Only *the name of Jesus* beats this with ten columns and a half (eight and a half for God), tied with the verb "to want" (*vouloir*), surprising at first in a specialist of that abandonment wherein one might see at times a danger of quietism, of being easy-going. Little Thérèse knew what she wanted. Her will was wholly bent towards Love and by it.

Although it seems now very old, the first book published on Thérèse after *The Story of a Soul* clearly brought out this primacy of Love. It is simply *L'Esprit de Sainte Thérèse d'après ses écrits et les témoins oculairs de sa vie (The Spirit of Saint Thérèse according to her Writings and the Eyewitnesses of her Life)*, published in 1923. From the title and the old-fashioned illustrations, one might think this some pious period art-craft on the background of Thérèse's writings. Not at all. If we go back without any previous assumptions to this book made up mostly of quotations, we see that her contemporaries, practically her sisters, who had gathered what they found best, in the final count went straight to the point. Of course their work was unscientific, they can be reproached for the subjectiveness of certain choices, and for many breaks, but surely their little sister was guiding their work . . . for their period, and according to the means they had.

Would not many controversies over Thérèse's writings subside if each one joined her where she wished to be, that is, in love? There may she gather all her friends, she who would have us be an "angel of peace and not a justice of the peace." (*Cons. et souv.*, p. 106)

This is only parenthetical, a small allotment to

controversy. . . . The source of everything, Thérèse's sisters were telling us back in 1923, is love. The way of childhood is only one aspect (in ch. 3), whereas the saint's virtues are the concrete expression of that integral love, with a well-deserved special mention of her simplicity (ch. 2). Even though this testimony throws off those fond of precise references, it has its value. We might also note that after years of research and of papers, the latest edition of her Manuscripts resumes the outline and the title of the first *Histoire d'une âme*. (Editions du Cerf)

Now as before, beyond the whole human context surrounding the childhood and the religious life of Saint Thérèse of the Child Jesus, what still counts is what God wanted to say through her to our times.

Now why through her? How was she prepared for this mission? This is a normal question for us to ask. The answer is given by Thérèse herself at the beginning of her first manuscript: "Jesus, going up on a mountain, called unto Himself *those He would*." (Mk 3:13) (Ms A, folio 2)

God's choices always contain an element of mystery. Thus Thérèse's commentary on Saint Mark's verse (3, 13): "This is the mystery of my vocation, of my whole life, and above all the mystery of Jesus' privileges on my soul. . . He does not call those who are worthy, but those whom He wills, or as Saint Paul says, God has pity on whom He wills, and He is merciful to whom He will be merciful. It is then not the work of him who wills nor of him who runs, but of God Who shows His mercy."

In all the studies undertaken on Thérèse, there is not one in which is not felt a profound and sincere love for the little saint, a true desire to know her better, to make her thoroughly known, to penetrate deeper into the mystery of this choice of God's, but something will always remain humanly inexplainable . . .

Back in 1951, Abbé Combes, the first to pioneer in the scientific study of Thérèse's works, raised the question of what would become of "history the day it would treat, just as Saint Thérèse of the Child Jesus treated it, the relation of love uniting Jesus to the holy Carmelite of Lisieux." He immediately replied, "It seems we can, without being over-imprudent, answer now. On that day history will at last understand Thérèse such as she is. It will understand that Saint Thérèse of Lisieux is in herself the realization of a definite program, fully contained in this quite unambiguous statement: 'I would so want to love Jesus, love Him more than He has ever been loved.'"

By reducing her spiritual life to this program, but giving it such powerful intensity, Thérèse rediscovered the essence of religious life, which adds up to nothing else but love's total adhesion to Jesus Christ. [*L'amour de Jésus chez Sainte Thérèse de Lisieux (Love of Jesus in Saint Thérèse of Lisieux)*].

Now what if renewal of religious life, so widely sought after, were here first of all? Right here?

"Oh, how little the good Lord is loved on earth! . . . even priests and religious . . . No, God is not much loved . . ." (CJ, Aug. 7)

1

My Vocation Is Love

It is not hard to see that from one end of her life to the other, Thérèse is lifted up by love, by love of God. From the first pages of her first manuscript right to the last lines of her three major writings, including her letters, her act of offering, her poems, and the notes taken by her sisters at her bedside, it is always the same movement. How can one help being struck by this?

"I loved God very much," she says in relating her very first memories. Thus, after her first communion: "I also felt the desire of loving God, of finding joy but in Him." (Ms A, folio 36) One must go back and reread with what fervor she prepared for this first communion. . . . No doubt she was privileged and satiated in this area (some will say a bit worked up!) as few children, very few children on earth, but God is free in His gifts, and it was for

His whole Church that He was preparing this choice ground. Thérèse bears witness to this plainly: *"You know, O my God, I have never desired but to love You, I have no ambition for any other glory. Your love has anticipated me from my infancy, it has grown with me, and now it is an abyss whose depth I cannot fathom . . ."* (Ms C, folio 35)

To say this about one's self! Yet it is true: when we arrive at the end of her life, that "course of a giant," at once broad and brief, only twenty-four years, Thérèse indeed no longer desires but one single grace, that this life "be broken by love." (Ms C, folio 8)

She repeats herself at the end of each one of her large manuscripts:

* Manuscript A, abounding in joy at Céline's entrance into Carmel: "I no longer have any desire except to love Jesus to the point of folly . . . Nor do I desire suffering or death, and yet I love both, but love alone draws me." (Ms A, folio 82)

* In Manuscript C, there is a shade of difference: "I no longer have any great desires except that of loving to the point of dying of love." (Ms C, folio 7) Her death being very near, Thérèse no longer says only that she has but one desire, of loving Jesus to the point of folly, for the mode of this mad love has defined itself, the road has been staked out, the way of death. So, it will be a death of love.

"I want to be a saint," she wrote to Mother Agnès de Jésus, March 27, 1888, at the age of fifteen. In this way too she aimed to be the glory of her father: "Yes, I shall remain forever your little queen. I shall endeavor to be your glory by becoming a great saint." (LT, May-June, 1888) She was then in Carmel since April 9th. We find on other occasions, especially in the years 1888-1889, this attraction towards sainthood, but not any kind: a great saint! Holiness, love are all one for Thérèse. She had long ago understood that "all is vanity and affliction of spirit under the sun . . . that the sole good is to love God with all one's heart and to be here below poor in spirit." (Ms A, folio 32) At twelve she knew, having tasted a few worldly amusements which she admits were not without their charm for this coquettish little bourgeois who found pleasure in showing off a new hat on Christmas Day, 1887, in spite of the pain of not being able to enter Carmel as fast as she wanted to. "Would you believe," she would later tell Céline, "that in spite of the ocean of bitterness I was plunged in, I was nevertheless glad to show off my pretty blue hat, adorned with a white dove! How strange these recoils of nature!" (*Cons. et souv.*, p. 24)

It is within a few months of this period that she becomes enthused over Abbé Arminjon's conferences on the future life: "Seeing there was no proportion between the rewards of eternal life and the slight sacrifices of life. I wanted *to love, to love* Jesus passionately, to give Him a thousand marks of affection while I still could . . . I incessantly repeated the words of love which had inflamed my heart . . ." (Ms A, folio 47) These were "assaults of love," of which she speaks much later to Mother Agnès taking down notes at her bedside, assaults of love which prepared the ground for that burst of flame, her act of offering to merciful love, and for the grace which followed shortly afterward: "From the age of fourteen, I did have these assaults of love. How I loved God! But it was nothing like after my act of offering. It was not a true flame which burned me." (CJ, July 17)

Mother Agnès had her relate it (a second time, for, notes Thérèse, the first time she had not paid attention):

"Well, I was beginning my way of the Cross when suddenly I was seized with so violent a love of God that I can only explain it by saying that it was as though I had been totally plunged into fire. O what fire and at the same time what sweetness! I burned with love, and I felt that one minute, one second more, I could not have stood such ardor without dying. I understood then what the saints say of these states which they have so often experienced. For myself I experienced it only once and only for an instant, then I fell back into my habitual dryness." (CJ, July 7)

What took place? No doubt it would have to be experienced to explain it. . . . But anyway, is there not here a kind of consecration by God Himself of the whole orientation of Thérèse's life? For this act of offering had a very precise and perfectly formulated purpose:

"In order to live in an act of perfect love . . ."

For years she asked for "love, infinite love with no other limit but You . . . Love which might be no longer me but You, Jesus." (profession note, Sept. 8, 1890)

Her ambition here was boundless: "I wish so much to love Him! . . .

To love Him more than He has ever been loved!" (LT, to Sister Agnès de Jésus, during her retreat for the taking of the habit, Jan. 6, 1889)

One day, she found how to fulfill this mad need: by that plunge into the infinite mercy of the Father. Immediately she composed her "act," that is she translated into words the fire which devoured her, she sweeps Céline along after, having quickly obtained permission from Mother Agnès, who does not understand very well what is happening, or at least seems not to attach much importance to this pious gesture among others. Yet it was the fruit of a long and fervent quest.

Already some months before, during Forty Hours, Feb. 26, 1895, she had poured forth her heart in one of those poems, whose form we have a right to dispute, but which are a very precious reflection of her deepest aspirations. Fifteen stanzas flow from Saint John's verse: "If anyone love me, he will keep my word, my Father will love him, and we will come to him and make our dwelling in him." (Jn 14:23) It is easy to imagine Thérèse in adoration before the Blessed Sacrament, turning over and ruminating the words of Jesus around the theme which obsesses her: "To live by Love."

"To live by Love, this is my heaven . . . this is my destiny" means what? Each stanza tries to answer, each answers some aspect, some color of the love Thérèse aspires after and which she would live by from day to day, including that dream of dying of love which recurs often elsewhere . . . and which is not far from coming true.

Naturally, she must begin by restating this love:

"Ah, you know, divine Jesus, I love You! . . .

Your gaze alone is my beatitude."

To live by love for Thérèse is first of all to live the life of God Who is Love, but will also be to "banish all fear":

"Of my sins I see no mark
In one sole instant love has burnt all!"

To live by Love is again "to look upon the Cross as a treasure," it is "to give without measure," it is "to sow peace and joy in every heart," it is finally to pray for priests, the Church, sinners:

"O God of Love, may they return to Your grace
And bless Your name forever."

We shall need to return to each of these aspects which recur in many other poems, but what gives them their unity, what impels Thérèse irresistably, is the thirst of love burning her.

"To love: how well made is our heart for this! . . . At times, I look for another word to express love, but in this land of exile, words are powerless to express all the soul's vibrations, so we must limit ourselves to this single word: To love! . . ." (LT, to Marie Guérin, July, 1890)

These lines she wrote five years before her act of offering, seven years before Manuscript B, that admirable letter to Sister Marie du Sacré-Coeur in which we can no longer have any doubts on the nature of that great movement lifting Thérèse, and with her lifting the world around her, the world to be, and all those souls who will live by her doctrine, all those who will join in this contest of Love.

"Give me a point to rest on," said Archimedes, "and with a lever I shall lift up the world." (Ms C, folio 36).

Thérèse herself quoted the great scholar a few weeks before dying. She too found a means to lift the world, love, more precisely "prayer (*oraison*) kindled by a fire of love." (Ms C, *ibid.*)

It is impossible to recopy here all of Manuscript B, which the most competent authorities testify is one of the masterpieces of spiritual literature. Thérèse literally burned, even though in her faith. Her sister Marie made no mistake when she replied, thanking her with much feeling, "Do you want me to tell you? Well, you are possessed by the good Lord, but possessed just as the wicked are said to be by the Evil One." (Letter to Thérèse, Sept., 1896)

That is correct. God-directed from her infancy, Thérèse very early experienced that the surest means of attaining God and of pleasing Him was love. She never to the end of her life wavered from this conviction: "I understand so well that only love can make us agreeable to God that this love is the only good I strive for . . ." (Ms B, folio 1)

She searched Scripture to satisfy her ardent desires and found at last that this love, which was her whole life, was her very vocation, a universal and most rewarding vocation. Who doesn't know these lines?

"I understood that the Church had a heart and that this heart was *burning with love*. I understood that Love alone made the members of the Church act, that if love ever burned out, the Apostles would no longer proclaim the gospel, martyrs would refuse to shed their blood . . . I understood that Love contained all vocations, that Love was all, embracing all times and all places . . . in a word it is eternal. . ."

"Then, in the excess of my delirious joy, I cried out, O Jesus, my Love, ... at last I have found my vocation, my vocation is LOVE! ... Yes, I have found my place in the Church: You, O my God, have given me that place ... in the heart of the Church, Mother, I shall be Love ... thus I shall be all ... thus my dreams will come true!!!" (Ms B, folio 3)

When Thérèse wrote this she still had a little over a year to live. Until the end she would repeat that love alone counts. Death did not frighten her: she never gave God anything but love, she was sure He would render her love and that love would all of a sudden break the cloth of her life without wearing it: "Break the cloth of this dear encounter. I have always applied those words to the death of love I desire. Love will not wear the cloth of my life, it will break it all of a sudden." (CJ, July 27)

On June 6, 1897, she cleverly replied to Sister Marie de la Trinité, who had asked her whether she felt any joy in going to paradise, "I would have very much if I went, but . . . I do not count on sickness, it is too slow a driver. " (In fact, she was to wait some four months longer.) "I no longer count but on love. Ask our good Jesus that all the prayers offered for me go to increasing the fire that is to consume me."

In the preface to *Derniers Entretiens (Last Conversations)*, it is said that Thérèse was unbelievably "in love with God." (Edition du Centenaire) Exactly. What mysterious inspiration, what urge was deposited in the heart of this young girl, what secret power?

It is the lever of Love, which can lift us too, and with us lift the Church and the world. For a resting point, God, and God alone! A mad ambition. Perhaps. But who would not want to end one's life as Thérèse ends her first manuscript, singing "the ever new hymn of Love"; (Ms A, folio 84) as she ends the second, belonging to that legion of souls "worthy of Love"; and finally as she ends the last, when from exhaustion her pen drops from her hands: in trust and in Love. (Ms C, folio 37)

2

To Love Jesus and
to Make Him Loved

Love then oriented Thérèse's whole life, almost from the cradle. As is normal, this love unfolded in many discoveries, and many consequences have been discovered, but in seeing flow all these streams, we must never forget their sole Source: GOD, the love of God first, the quest for Him before all.

Thérèse noted this when speaking of her role as mistress of novices, a situation which probably prevailed from the very beginning of her religious life: "I sensed that the one thing necessary was to unite more and more with Jesus, and that the rest would be given me over and above." (Ms C, folio 22)

Her only Friend:

At the age of twelve, after her first communion, Jesus was her "only Friend." For Thérèse, by the way, God was often "*le bon Dieu,*" but still more often just simply "Jesus." She had to go back to the abbey where she had gone to school and which she had to leave because of her poor health, physical and nervous. She came back and joined the Children of Mary, hence her rather peculiar situation amidst the other children. "No one paid any attention to me, so I went up to the choir loft and remained before the Blessed Sacrament until Papa came to get me. This was my only consolation. Was not Jesus my only Friend?" . . . (Ms A, folio 40)

Writing these lines some ten years later, Saint Thérèse of the Child Jesus recognized in her child's heart the only love she still had and which she would describe in the same way one year before her death, "O Jesus, my first, my only Friend, I love you alone." (Ms B, folio 4)

That she was favored in her family as few children ever are, makes no difference. If she intensely loved those in her family, and was fondly endeared by them, the great Love residing deep in her heart was the Love of God.

She stated this also in relating her trip to Rome: "Religious life appeared to me as it is, with its servitudes, its small sacrifices accomplished in the shadows. I understood how easy it is to withdraw into one's self, to forget the sublime purpose of one's vocation, and I said to myself: later, in the hour of trial, when a prisoner of Carmel, unable to contemplate but a tiny corner of the starry sky, I shall remember what I see today; this thought will give me courage, I shall easily forget my poor little interests on seeing the grandeur and the power of the God I wish alone to serve." (Ms A, folio 58)

Incidentally, one can admire the maturity of this child of fifteen, yet so "childlike" in other ways, who had so well foreseen the kind of life awaiting her that on June 9, 1897, she could repeat the same thing, her essential course unmoved except to gain in stress: "Dear little brother, about to appear before God, I understand more than ever that there is only one thing necessary, to work solely for Him . . ." (LT, to Abbé Bellière)

So to work with an amazing fervor, as though this concentration on God alone had increased tenfold her ability to love, which is indeed the first fruit of contemplative life. The flame burning her reaches its utmost expression when she sets before Sister Marie du Sacré-Coeur her desire for martyrdom. In this famous page's indisputable urge of the spirit, there is indeed an uplift, even though one is tempted to think in the back of one's mind that one kind of martyrdom would suffice! Here as elsewhere for Thérèse there is no limit.

"Martyrdom, the dream of my youth; this dream has grown with me under the cloisters of Carmel . . . But here again I sense that my dream is madness, for I could not limit myself to one kind of martyrdom . . . to be satisfied I would need them all . . . As You, my adorable Spouse, I would be scourged and crucified . . . I would want to die flayed like Saint Bartholomew . . . Like Saint John I would want to be plunged into boiling oil, I would want to undergo all the tortures inflicted on the martyrs. With Saint Agnes and Saint Cecilia, I would want to bare my neck to the sword, and like Saint Joan of Arc, my darling sister, I would want to murmur your name, *O Jesus*, at the stake . . . When I think of the torments that will be the lot of Christians in the days of the antichrist, I feel my heart quiver and I would want these torments to be reserved for me . . . *Jesus, Jesus*, if I wanted to write down all my desires, I would have to borrow your book of life, in which are related the deeds of all the saints, and these deeds I would want to have accomplished for You . . ." (Ms B, folio 3)

Jesus, Jesus, Jesus. This name recurs three times. This is no adolescent girl's infatuation for heroism—she proved this, it is a thrust of total and exclusive love of God, madly ambitious.

To make Him loved as I love Him:

Yet this exclusiveness in the love of God, an exclusiveness allowable only with God, is an exclusiveness . . . which does not exclude, precisely because it concerns God.

The purity of Thérèse's love of God, its absoluteness, cannot help but strike, yet it is not a closed *tête-à-tête*. Very far from it! On the contrary, Thérèse's love broadens with a new desire which seems indeed to be the clearest sign of this purity itself.

It is not the joy of sharing this love with others, although she knew this and aspired to it; nor is it directly love of neighbor, very present in Thérèse, but as an overflow and normal sequel of that extraordinary love of God, with which it was all one. It was a zeal for God Himself, a zeal which would bring about all the others: the desire *to make Him loved, loved for Himself first.*

This is not immediately noticeable in Thérèse's writings, nor was Thérèse herself immediately aware of this. This desire was not expressed before 1889, hence not before the age of sixteen, but which at the end of her life is never separated from her desire to love God Himself. This is very striking, especially in her letters.

After the famous miracle of Christmas, the desire "to work for the conversion of sinners" was lit in her, a desire she says she had never felt so vividly. (Ms A, folio 45) Thus it already existed, but less strong, less conscious. "I sensed in a word, charity entering my heart, the need of forgetting myself to please, and from then on I was happy."

This was a true conversion, not to be taken lightly. The little spoiled child of Lisieux truly had a discovery to make in self-forgetting, but this is not what she would write to Céline on October 15, 1889. (Let us recall that she had been in Carmel around a year and a half.) "There is only one thing we can do at night, the sole night of life, which will occur once, and that is to love, to love Jesus with all the strength of our heart and to save souls for Him *in order that He be loved*. Oh, to make Jesus loved!"

The apostolic urge at its purest: to be an apostle with the intent to do good to one's neighbor, with the intent to make God known to him, His goodness, His love, His life. This is all very fine and beautiful, the sign of true faith and of a great love for one's brethren, for this is truly the best that can be revealed and given to them. But a view such as Thérèse's extends still further, because it starts from the very source: she is an apostle for God Himself, first of all, and this requires loving the Lord a great deal, to be possessed to this point with desire to make Him loved.

Thérèse's love went far beyond the desire of being loved by Him or of experiencing His love, that so subtle and so current deviation of prayer life: whoever has tried in the least to pray could not help but understand this! It was likewise beyond the legitimate joy of apostolic activity in which one gives to others the best of one's self, but which, as everyone knows, can easily degenerate into activism, that form of spiritual sloth in which one can with the finest of reasons wind up being so much one's self. Her passion is truly the glory of God: that He be everywhere known, loved and glorified. She had expressed this orientation in all its somewhat mad purity before her entry into Carmel, shortly after a quite cooling visit with Monsieur Delatroëtte, the superior who regarded without enthusiasm such a young girl entering the cloister.

"One evening, unable to tell Jesus that I loved Him and how much I desired that He be *everywhere loved and glorified*, I reflected painfully that He could never receive from hell one single act of love; then I told God that to please Him I would willingly consent to being plunged into hell, in order that He might eternally be loved in this place of blasphemy." (Ms A, folio 52)

Evidently we are in another key from social justice or humanitarian projects which characterize our times. We do not here intend to diminish their value in any way, but what true believer would dare think or say that such a view of God Himself, for

Himself, does not embrace the whole planet and beyond, although in a different way?

The whole of Thérèse's texts on the matter from 1896 on, must be read consecutively, exclusively in her *Letters* (which does not mean there is nothing elsewhere in this sense). We have selected ten of them.

After the Manuscripts, which best reflect Thérèse's soul (particularly B and C, because she was really conscious of having a message to deliver and because there she said what she wanted to say for those who would read her), her Letters are also a mine for a good knowledge of her, especially those letters in which she discloses her innermost feelings, to her brother priests, Céline, Mother Agnès, etc.

Here then is the first text, to Father Roulland, on June 23, 1896, before his ordination:

"I beg you, Reverend Father, ask Jesus for me, on the day He will deign for the first time to come down from heaven at the sound of your voice, ask Him to inflame me with the fire of His Love so that I may then help you to light it in hearts."

On November 1, 1896, she wrote to this same Father Roulland:

"I did not know that for six years (Footnote: Thérèse had just discovered that on the very day of her profession, on September 8, 1890, when she asked 'that in her stead a priest might receive those graces of the Lord, that he have the same aspirations, the same desires as she . . . ,' Father Roulland's missionary vocation had been saved by Mary.) I had a brother who was preparing to become a missionary. Now that this brother is actually His apostle, Jesus has revealed to me this mystery in order no doubt to increase in my heart the desire *to love Him and to make Him loved . . .*"

"You promise me, Brother, to continue to say each morning at the holy altar: 'My God, inflame my sister with your love.' "

To Brother Siméon, on January 27, 1897:

"The only thing I pray you to ask for my soul is the grace to love *Jesus* and *to make Him loved* as much as I can."

On February 24, 1897, she wrote to Abbé Bellière in exactly the same terms:

"United in Him, our souls will be able to save many others for this dear Jesus said, 'If two of you agree together, whatever they ask my Father shall be granted to them. . .' Ah! what we ask of Him is to work for His glory, *to love Him and to make Him loved . . .*"

This is the letter to Abbé Bellière in which we find the prayer quoted in our introduction and which it is not superfluous to reread in its context:

"You tell me that very often you pray for your sister. Since you are this charitable, I would be happy if you consented to recite daily for her this prayer which contains all her desires: 'Merciful Father, in the name of our Sweet Jesus, of the Virgin Mary and of the saints, I ask you to inflame my sister with the Spirit of Love and to grant her *the grace of making You greatly loved.*' You promised me to pray for me all your life. No doubt it will be longer than mine, so you are not allowed to sing as I do, 'My hope is, my exile will be short,' but you are not allowed to forget your promise. If the Lord soon takes me with Him, I ask you to continue daily this same little prayer, for in heaven I shall desire the same as on earth, *to love Jesus and to make Him loved.*"

Thus Thérèse is far from seeing heaven solely and primarily as the time and place for finding again at last family intimacy. It is true she does speak of this repeatedly in this sense, particularly in Manuscript A:

" 'Life is your ship, not your dwelling.' . . . When I was tiny these words gave me courage. Does not wisdom say that 'Life is like a ship which splits the choppy waves and leaves after it no trace of its rapid passage?' . . . When I think of this, my soul plunges into the infinite, I seem to touch already the eternal shore . . . I seem to be embraced by Jesus . . . I think I see my heavenly mother coming to meet me with Papa, Mama, and the four little angels . . . I think I enjoy at last forever true, everlasting family life . . ." (Ms A, folio 41)

This indeed was Thérèse writing all that, but it would be untrue to so limit her desires for the beyond, when is known her intent, so positively stated, to "spend her heaven doing good on earth." (CJ, July 17) This very definite orientation recurs in a letter written to Father Roulland on March 19, 1897:

"I do hope, dear Brother, that if I left this exile, you will not forget your promise to pray for me. You have always received my requests with so much kindness that I dare again to make another. I do not desire that you ask God to deliver me from the flames of purgatory. Saint Teresa used to say to her daughters, 'What do I care if I stay in purgatory until the end of the world, if my prayers save a single soul!' These words echo in my heart: I would save souls and forget myself for them. I would want to save them even after my death. So I would be glad if you then said, instead of the little prayer you recite and which would forever be answered: 'my God, allow my sister *to make You still loved!*' If Jesus hears and answers you, I will find a way to prove you my gratitude."

On April 25th, she repeats herself again, this time to Abbé Bellière, a young hypersensitive priest who truly received the saint's last confidences, no doubt because he needed them more than the others:

"In the solitude of Carmel, I have understood that my mission was not to have crowned a mortal king (*Footnote:* Like Joan of Arc, whom Thérèse loved greatly), but *to make the King of Heaven loved*, to subject to Him the kingdom of hearts."

A few days later, on May 2nd, she wrote to quite a different person, a sister she knew well, Anne du Sacré-Coeur. This message was headed for Saigon. "Please, Sister, I beg you to ask Jesus *that I also might love Him and make Him loved.* I would want to love with no ordinary love but as the saints who performed for Him deeds of madness. Alas, how far I am from resembling them! . . . Ask Jesus too that I may always do His will. For this I am ready to cross the world . . . I am also ready to die!"

The last two quotations are also extracted from letters to her spiritual brothers, July 14th to Fr. Roulland, and August 10th, her very last letter written on earth, very moving, to Abbé Bellière.

July 14th:

"I do not expect to remain inactive in heaven. My desire is to keep on working for the Church and souls. I ask God this and I am sure He will grant it . . . What draws me to the heavenly homeland is God's call, the hope of *at last loving Him as I have so desired* and the thought that I shall be able *to make Him loved* by a multitude of souls who will bless Him eternally."

August 10th:

"To God (*A Dieu*, in two words), dear little

Brother, May He grant us the grace of *loving Him and of saving souls for Him*. Your unworthy sister makes this wish."

Thérèse could most truly testify for herself, as related by Mother Agnès:

"I am not selfish, I love God, not myself . . ." (CJ, July 27)

Who led Thérèse along this way? Jesus Himself, "her only director," as she has said. Yet, a certain influence of Father Pichon, universal counsellor of the Martin family, comes to mind when reading one of his letters, dated March 27, 1890. By then Thérèse has been at Carmel for two years and is seventeen: "Do not be content with loving Jesus, you must make Him loved. Would you be without this a daughter of Saint Teresa? Now, to love Jesus, it is necessary to suffer, to suffer much . . ."

Such an appeal could not help but echo immediately and generously in Thérèse, including the conditions of fulfillment, to suffer, to suffer much. For Thérèse was possessed with the desire to make Jesus loved, and to suffer anything for this. This is the gospel, the clear and sure way of the Cross: If anyone will come after me. . . . Not a dream of static contemplation, but a basic aspiration to enter the grand current of the love of God for men. This follows Saint Dominic (who is said to have spoken only to or about God), who also asked his sons and daughters to be convinced "that they would only be truly members of Christ the day they would give themselves totally to win souls, as the Lord Jesus, Savior of all men, offered Himself completely in oblation for our salvation." (Jordan of Saxony, *Libellus*, no. 13)

Then again, to see one's self so poor in loving the Lord, so powerless; how consoling and how invigorating to think that this very poverty and the suffering which sometimes results from it can, if accepted, contribute to having loved the One to Whom one intended to give all. If we do not know how, and are unable to love Him as we would like to, at least might we make Him loved! And this "least" contains in itself a fullness and a wonderful source of joy.

If we happen to fall, to offend our Love, Thérèse, as we shall see later, will have further resources available as usual to all, thanks to her "way of trust."

She wrote to Abbé Bellière on June 21, 1897: "Do not think I blame you for repenting for your faults and for your desire to expiate them. Oh, no! I am far from this, but, you know, now we are two, the work will be done faster and I, in my way, will do more work than you."

A few lines before: "I try not to be concerned about myself anymore at all, and what Jesus deigns to accomplish in my soul I abandon to Him, for I have not chosen an austere life to expiate my faults, but those of others."

She was not the one to commit herself as Zacchaeus did: "If I have wronged anyone, I will restore it fourfold." Unless a great deal has been stolen, where can this fourfold be drawn from? No matter, for in the treasures of divine mercy there will be far more!

How and what to do in order "to make Jesus loved," particularly in a life which does not imply "works"? It would not be difficult to draw a long list. Everyone knows there is a way of life which does not make God loved and does not make one feel like wanting to know Him: whatever betrays brotherly love and in particular truth. I prefer to let do Father Pichon's remark: "Now, to make Jesus loved, requires a great deal of suffering . . ."

Only, this throws light on suffering.

Those you have given me:

It is clear that in Thérèse the zeal to make her Lord loved and *love of others* are all one, since the best way of loving them is to want before all else to see them love the Lord, and that true brotherly love is the surest means to lead one's neighbor to God.

Here quotations proliferate, and very early at that.

The story of Pranzini, her "first child," is known by all, as is her earnestness in praying for priests, especially from the time of her trip to Rome on. This is one of the special reasons she gave for her entering Carmel. Until the end of her life, she would pray for a Carmelite, Father Hyacinthe Loyson, who had left the religious life in particularly painful circumstances. She would offer for him her last communion, August 10, 1897.

On July 23, 1891, at the age of eighteen, she cried out, "Ah, Céline, we must not forget souls, we must forget ourselves for them!"

On August 15, 1892, again to Céline: "Jesus' love for us is so incomprehensible that He wishes us to share with Him in saving souls. He wishes to do nothing without us. The Creator of the universe awaits the prayer of a poor little soul to save the other souls redeemed like itself at the cost of His blood. Our own vocation is not to go harvest in the fields of ripe wheat. Jesus does not say to us, 'Lower your eyes, look at the countryside and go harvest.' Our mission is yet more sublime. Here is what our Jesus says to us, 'Lift up your eyes and see.' See how in my heaven there are empty places: you are to fill them. You are my Moseses praying on the mountain. Ask me for workers and I will send them. I await but a prayer, a sigh from your heart! . . . Is not the apostolate of prayer so to speak higher than that of the word? Our mission as

Carmelites is to train evangelical workers who will save thousands of souls of whom we shall be mothers . . . Céline, were these not the very words of our Jesus, who would dare believe them? . . . I find our lot so beautiful. What have we to envy in priests? . . . How I wish I could tell you all that is on my mind, but I am short of time: understand all I cannot write you! . . ."

Certainly, in her correspondence to her brother priests, she dreamt only of helping them in their apostolic task: "I hope, Monsieur l'Abbé, that our dear Jesus will make your grand desires come true. I ask Him that you might be not only a good missionary but a saint all afire with the love of God and of souls: I beg you to obtain for me too this love so that I can help you in your apostolic undertaking. A Carmelite, you know, who would not be an apostle would stray from the purpose of her vocation and cease to be a daughter of Seraphic Saint Teresa, who desired to give a thousand lives to save a single soul." (LT, to Abbé Bellière, October 21, 1896)

In life hereafter, as we have already seen, the same view, the same desire to be an apostle: "If I go to purgatory I shall be very glad! I shall do as the three Hebrews in the furnace, I shall stroll amid the flames singing the canticle of Love. Oh, how happy I would be if in going to purgatory, I could liberate other souls, suffer in their stead, for then I would be doing good, I would be freeing captives!" (CJ, July 8)

The desire "to spend her heaven doing good on earth," she uttered very shortly before her death, when she was exhausted and might have aspired only to be delivered. "My mission is to make God loved as I love Him, to give souls my little way. If my wishes are granted, my heaven will be spent on earth till the end of the world. Yes, I want to spend my heaven doing good on earth." (CJ, July 17)

One might wonder whether there are many Christians, even those fervent, even those very "committed," even in the contemplative life wherein God's interests in principle take all the place, who regard beatitude in this way and count on eternal rest only "when the number of the elect is complete." . . . (CJ, July 17)

Zeal for the salvation of souls, for universal beatitude, in Thérèse culminates in two summits:

The first summit: in her ardent missionary longings expressed especially through Manuscript B to Sister Marie du Sacré-Coeur: "Ah, in spite of my littleness, I would want to enlighten souls as the prophets and doctors! I have the vocation to be an apostle . . . I would want to travel around the globe, preach Your Name and plant on infidel ground Your glorious Cross, but O my Beloved! one mission would not be enough, I would want to proclaim the gospel at the same time on the five continents and to the farthermost islands . . . I would want to be a missionary not only during a few years, but I would want to have been since the creation of the world and be to the end of time . . . But I would want above all, O my beloved Savior, I would want to shed my blood for you to the last drop . . ." (Ms B, folio 3)

This she did in her hemoptyses.

This missionary ardor blended very well with her life of prayer, which she did not want to fulfill otherwise, she who before entering the convent barred herself from reading missionary magazines so as not to arouse her desires, knowing full well that God was calling her to fulfill them in Carmel. She too it was who, when she showed a longing to leave for Saigon, specified that it was not to render any great services: "I would be glad to go to Hanoi to suffer greatly for God. I would want to go to be all alone, to have no consolation on earth. As for being useful over there, the thought does not even occur to me. I know very well I would do nothing at all." (CJ, May 15) "My only purpose would be to accomplish God's will, to sacrifice myself for Him." (Ms C, folio 10)

The second summit: to eat at the table of sinners, again in Manuscript C. Thérèse spoke to Mother Marie de Gonzague about the trial of her faith. She meditated long that *light came into the world and the darkness did not receive it.*

"But, Lord, Your child has understood this divine light of Yours, she asks pardon for her brothers, she accepts to eat the bread of sorrow as long as You wish and does not want to rise from this table filled with bitterness, at which poor sinners eat, until the day you have marked . . ."

"But also, can she not say in her name and in the name of her brothers: Have mercy on us, Lord, for we are poor sinners! O Lord, send us away justified! . . . May all those not enlightened by the luminous torch of faith at least see it . . . O Jesus, if the table soiled by them must be purified by a soul who loves You, I shall be glad to eat there alone the bread of trial until it is Your good pleasure to let me into Your bright kingdom. The only grace I ask of you is never to offend You! . . ." (Ms C, folio 6)

These are strong words, especially since they were written in the very midst of trial, and have been called attention to by many authors. Thérèse knew what she was talking about, but what love, what extraordinary training in love had ever prepared this strength of soul so that in the middle of the storm she might turn to her Beloved? Job had not done so much, nor had Jehovah blamed him for it.

That is not all. Thérèse writes on: "So it is that in spite of this trial which takes away all enjoyment, I can still cry out: 'Lord, You fill me with *joy* by everything You do!' For is there any greater joy than to suffer for Your love? The more inward the suffering, the less it appears to the eyes of creatures, the more it gladdens You, O my God! But if impossibly You were not to know of my suffering, I would still be happy to have it if I could thereby prevent or repair a single fault committed against faith." (Ms C, folio 7)

This is fire! May it burn us also. It is impossible without a great inner passion to improvise such a page on a mere literary level. Here we have a purity of love of God, and of neighbor deriving from God, which seems hard to surpass. But not to be discouraged by so great an incentive, we who in smaller trials have much less, must reread *Derniers entretiens* (Last Conversations) and see how this practically natural heroism blended with a life attitude so simple, so human, ultimately so accessible. Thérèse fully discovered, only in the last year of her life, the new commandment, purity of love for God. The new commandment, in concrete life, was with people who surrounded her every day.

Here we would have to reread all the last part of Manuscript C, from folio 11 to 35, but we shall select the most significant passages.

"This year, dear Mother, God made me understand what charity is. True, I understood it before, but imperfectly. I had not fully fathomed these words of Jesus: the second commandment is *simi-*

lar to the first: you shall love your neighbor as yourself. I endeavored to love God, and it is in loving Him that I understood that my love must not express itself only in words, for 'It is not those who say Lord, Lord! who will enter the kingdom of heaven, but those who do the will of God.' This will Jesus made known often, almost on every page of the gospel, but at the Last Supper, when He knew his disciples were burning with a more ardent love for the One Who had just given Himself to them in the ineffable mystery of His Eucharist, this dear Savior wanted to give them a new commandment. He said to them with inexpressible tenderness, 'I make for you a new commandment, that you mutually love one another, and that, *as I have loved you, you are to love one another*. The mark by which the world will recognize that you are my disciples is if you love one another.' " (Ms C, folio 11)

"This year" was the year of her death. This does not mean she understood nothing before—she made this clear, but a light dawned, and this came in sickness and trial, but particularly affected her outlook on God: "I tried above all to love God, and in loving Him (We have seen in what manner!) I understood, etc . . ."

"I tried above all to love God . . ." Thérèse was always at the source, the right one, the only true source, the one from which would necessarily spring the dynamic discovery of brotherly love.

Love of neighbor, genuine love of neighbor can take root only in love of God. With a right look on God, everybody can also hope to make a discovery of true brotherly love "before passing from this world to the Father."

Now what did Thérèse discover?

"I understood how much my love for my sisters was imperfect, I saw that I did not love them as God loves them. So! Now I understand that perfect charity consists in bearing others' faults, in not being astonished at their weaknesses, in being edified at the smallest acts of virtue we see them practise, but above all I understood that charity must not remain shut up in the bottom of one's heart: 'No one,' says Jesus, 'lights a torch to put it under a bushel, but he puts it on a candlestick, so that it will shine on *all* those in the house.' It seems to me this torch stands for the charity that should shine on and gladden not only those dearest to me, but *all* those in the house, without omitting anyone." (Ms C, folio 12)

Thérèse did not see her sisters through the haze which the common life sometimes casts on all the best. She was acquainted with "the lack of judgment, of education, the touchiness of certain characters, all things which do not make life very pleasant" (Ms C, folio 28), but she also understood that love of God is far beyond such weaknesses of nature.

"How did Jesus love His disciples, and why did He love them? Oh, it was not their natural qualities that could attract Him: there was between them and Him an infinite distance. He was Knowledge, eternal Wisdom, they were poor sinners, ignorant and filled with earthly thoughts. Nevertheless, Jesus called them His friends, His brothers. He wanted to see them reign with Him in the kingdom of His Father, and to open to them this kingdom, He wanted to die on a cross, for He said, 'there is no greater love than to give one's life for those one loves.' " (Ms C, folio 12)

We know too that Sister Thérèse taught her novices not to judge one's neighbor unfavorably. She for instance said to Céline "that one must always treat others with charity, for very often what seems negligence to our eyes is in the eyes of God heroic: a sister who has migraine or who suffers in her soul does more in accomplishing half her work than another healthy in body and mind and who does the whole thing." (cf. François de Ste-Marie, vol. II, p. 72)

To have the same view on one's neighbor as God, one must stand in Him. To love one's neighbor as God loves him is the new commandment, Thérèse's last discovery in the realm of Love.

"But above all, I understood that charity must not remain shut up in the bottom of one's heart." It is a duty to express this universal charity, to warm others with it. We should never meet anyone without wanting to warm him, not with our charity but with God's. This is possible only by remaining continually in Him, the One Who continually infuses in us the warmth of life, His Life.

"You well know that I could not love my sisters as You Yourself love them if You, O my Jesus, did not still love them in me . . . Yes, I feel that when I am charitable, it is Jesus alone acting in me. The more I am united with Him, the more I love all my sisters." (Ms C, folio 12)

One always returns to the source.

"Charity alone can expand my heart. O Jesus, since this dear flame consumes me, I run in the path of Your new commandment." (Ms C, folio 16)

Nor did Thérèse limit herself to principles, to "a kind of discourse on charity." (Ms C, folio 17) She gave examples of how to live it, related well-known recollections: how she succeeded so well in overcoming her antipathy for Sister Thérèse de Saint-Augustin, that "potted lily," that the latter wound up believing she was her favorite; how she used to desert, fleeing the scene of battle when she feared to succumb; and how she mastered the difficult art of rendering a service, as well as of asking humbly: thus one behaves "as the poor who stretch out their hand to receive what they need; if they are refused, they are not surprised, no one owes them anything." (Ms C, folio 16) However, more than details, even to be relished, we seek here above all the soul's movement, an uplifting movement; "Just as a torrent rushing impetuously into the ocean carries with it all it meets along its path, so too, O my Jesus, the soul which plunges into the shoreless ocean of Your love drags with it the treasures it contains." (Ms C, folio 34)

"To love Jesus" is indeed the only movement which lifts up Thérèse.

"To make Him loved" is to draw after her in this uplifting movement all the treasures she owns. Now she has no other treasures than the souls God has been pleased to join to hers: "For simple souls no complicated means are needed. Since I count among them, one morning during my thanksgiving, Jesus gave me a simple means of accomplishing my mission. He made me understand these words of the Canticle of Canticles: 'Draw me, we run in the scent of your perfumes.' O Jesus, it is not necessary to say, 'In drawing me, draw the souls I love.' Simply 'Draw me' suffices."

That is how Thérèse brings everything back to unity, to the sole love she is possessed by, a clear-eyed, appeasing love. Is it inaccessible to us? It would be discouraging, and so contrary to the grace proper to Thérèse, whose very purpose was to lay out a road for all, especially for the poorest, the weakest, the smallest.

There is one means to follow her, only one accessible to everyone, whatever their temperament, their past history and their present living conditions. That means is trust.

"I rise to Him by trust and love." These are Thérèse's very last words in her Manuscripts. Better yet, trust is the road of love, the only way by which this little Carmelite's purity of love might be imitated by us poor sinners, those run of the mill who nevertheless more or less dream of that extraordinary passion of love for God and, in Him, for all men.

3

The Way of Trust

Has not everything been said on Saint Thérèse of the Child Jesus' trust? Fearfully so, yet how can we speak of the love which devoured her, without at the same time stating that it is inseparable from trust? We cannot.

On the waves of trust and love:

For if love is the center of Thérèse's life, if she was possessed by the desire to love God and to make Him loved, this fiery love which inspires all saints is in her very personalized. It is rooted in *trust*, trust that "God cannot inspire unrealizable desires" (Ms C, folio 2), and above all trust in the midst of great weakness and of a real powerlessness, and in a climate which could only favor such a discovery.

We must reread Thérèse's first communion

retreat notes and see up close the fear of falling into mortal sin instilled into children! Nor was Carmel hardly any better. The counselling of Abbé Youf, who was the community's confessor during all of Thérèse's religious life, was not all expansive, and she certainly suffered from this, at least in the first years. In the latest edition of her Letters we read this remark: "One day when Thérèse admitted to her confessor her sorrow for suffering so much from despondency during Mass that she was unable to overcome sleep, he remonstrated her severely, telling her that she offended God." (Edition du Centenaire, p. 464)

The other religious were led by the same "energetic way." Thus, Sr. Thérèse de Saint-Augustin was dismissed one day with these encouraging words: "My poor child, all I can tell you is that you already have one foot in hell and that if you continue, you will soon put the second foot in." When this was confided to Mother Marie de Gonzague, she undisturbedly gave the following sympathetic answer: "Relax, I already have both in!"

"Yet Thérèse only grounded herself more and more in trust over the years, to the point of making it the heart of that little way so short and straight, so new." (Ms C, folio 2), which she felt charged by God to disclose to souls.

This must be clearly understood: trust with her is not merely a particular shade of love, as one might speak of a trustful love. It is the way which leads to the fullness of love. The center, we have clearly seen, is love. To attain it, a single means: trust. Trust—that one can attain it, but finally above all trust in God's infinite mercy, which will lift us to His very Self. Thérèse had this longing and conviction from way back, since she indeed expressed them in the first pages of Manuscript A when speaking of her adolescence: "I thought I was born for glory, and seeking the means to attain it God inspired in me the sentiments I just wrote of. He made me understand that my own glory would not appear to mortals, that it would consist in becoming a great saint!!! This desire might seem rash, considering how weak and imperfect I was, and how much I still am after spending six years in religion. Nevertheless, I still feel the same bold confidence of becoming a great saint, for, having no merits, I do not count on them, but I hope in the One Who is Virtue, Holiness Itself. He alone, satisfied with my weak efforts, will make me holy." (Ms A, folio 32)

This trust comes down to being nothing else but an extraordinary sense of God's goodness, the conviction that God is Love, a conviction pushed to the limit with great logic.

Sister Thérèse used to speak of her "way of trust." The expression "way of childhood" supplanted it only much later in the writing of Mother

Agnès, inclined, says the published *Derniers entre-tiens* (Last Conversations), to stress all her sister's virtues of childhood. This is important because this is what has made Thérèse's message so tasteless. It is true that the mark of childhood, of smallness, of the sense of nothingness before God is very clear in her, but it is subordinated to trust and love. It should not be thought that playing the child or taking refuge in a false brand of childhood will disclose Thérèse's way. We shall become aware of the values of true childhood before God in living by trust. The origin of Thérèse's discovery concerning her "little way" is trust. Because she thought that God in His infinite love could not inspire unrealiz-able desires, hence by virtue of a total trust in that God she loved more than anything, trust in the goodness of a Father unable to deceive His children. On account of all this Thérèse sought to fulfill at any price her desires for holiness.

How did she arrive for herself at so firm an assurance and so quiet a holiness? How can we in turn enter upon that way so well made to launch everyone?

First for Thérèse herself:

There was, as we have seen, a mysterious grace, a wholly gratuitous intuition into the depths of God's mercy, in a social background which hardly tended this way, even though within a family which did contribute much to her becoming aware of this intuition. The education she had received gives the impression that Thérèse could not do without trust and love. Raised in an atmosphere of tenderness, she was as if naturally sure of God's goodness, which everything from her early years told her of. Of course, the psychological resonances of such an environment can be discussed, and this hot-house climate can be not always comfortable, but we must recognize that as things were the family background did help Thérèse make her principal discoveries. She could not help giving a very strong sense of God's fatherhood, she could not help having in her heart an infinite thirst for love, of a boundless love, she who had been both tenderly rocked and rudely broken by separations. Her genius was to believe that this irresistable bent of her being could not help but lead to something immense, far beyond any family affections or privations. She recognized in her heart the very movement of God, and she believed in His Love with boundless trust.

This intuition was as it were consecrated in 1891 during a retreat preached by a Franciscan, Father Alexis Prou, who "launched her full sail upon the waves of trust and love."

"The good Lord, wanting to show me that He alone was my soul's director, used this very father whom I alone had appreciated . . . I then suffered great interior trials of all kinds (to the point of wondering at times whether there was a heaven). I felt disposed not to say anything of my intimate disposition, not knowing how to express them, but hardly in the confessional, I felt my soul expand. After having said few words, I was understood in a wonderful way, even guessed at . . . My soul was like a book out of which Father read better than I myself . . . He launched me full sail upon the waves of trust and love which were drawing me so strongly but on which I dared not advance . . ." (Ms A, folio 80)

Now she will dare, all the way!

Everyone dreams of trust, but not many, if I dare say so, dare let themselves go, lose themselves enough, accept no longer "holding their souls between their hands," to sail upon the waves of trust and love. Many say as Thérèse: "I am by nature such that fear makes me draw back; with love not only I advance but I fly." (*ibid.*) But who will pay the price of love to fly like her?

Regardless, Thérèse will no longer change her language to the end of her life, and her last letters, her last words are all loaded with a total trust and with a refusal to torture herself with anything at all. "We must go to heaven by the same way: suffering joined with love . . . I shall teach you how you are to navigate upon the stormy sea of the world: with abandonment and the love of a child who knows that his father cherishes him and could not leave him alone in the hour of danger . . . But why speak to you of the life of trust and love? I explain myself so poorly that I must wait for heaven to talk to you about this happy life."

This was addressed to Abbé Bellière July 18, 1897. About the same time, she had written a long letter to Father Pichon telling all God had done for her, all she thought of His love and His mercy, her hopes, her desire to do good on earth, and she based herself with commentary on psalm 23: "The Lord is my shepherd, nothing do I lack . . ."

Alas, if Thérèse kept Father Pichon's rare letters, he did not keep hers, so we no longer have that treasure which was to be as her final spiritual testament. Let us console ourselves with what she said elsewhere to Sr. Geneviève de la Sainte-Face, her Céline. This too is a short commentary of the same psalm: "O my God . . . now that you join external suffering to the trials of my soul, I cannot say 'The pangs of death surrounded me,' but I cry out in my thankfulness, 'I have gone down into the valley of the shadow of death, yet I fear no evil, because you are with me, Lord.' " (LT, August, 1897)

July 23rd she confided to Mother Agnès: "No, God does not give me a presentiment of imminent death, but of much greater sufferings . . . However, I do not torment myself, I only want to think of the present moment."

At the end of October, 1896, she wrote to Sister Marie de Saint-Joseph: "Near that Heart (the heart of Jesus), one learns valiantness and above all trust."

Finally, the last pages of her last Manuscript are totally suffused with trust. "I rise to Him by trust and Love." Could this message written by Thérèse have a better ending? Mother Agnès stated very precisely that nothing else was written on the page, "as one might think on seeing that it was cut short." Who would doubt it?

For us:

Saint Thérèse of the Child Jesus is said to be the imitable saint par excellence. Nothing extraordinary in her life. She herself boasted of doing nothing "little souls" could not do. She guarded against desiring "a beautiful death," unless it was to please her sisters, etc.

Was she ever aware though that the love lifting her up was properly inimitable? We can be filled with admiration and enthusiasm on reading of her ardent desire for all the forms of martyrdom, for instance, of her thirst to fulfill all the vocations in the Church in all places and at every moment, but how can this exclusive love of God, as strong as death, extraordinarily disinterested and tactful, ever be imitated? Who would ever think of wiping his brow on a hot day furtively before God alone, rather than in front of others, so as not to show

Him how bad off one is from what He sends? "God, Who loves us so much, is sorry enough to have to leave us on earth to fulfill our time of trial, without having us constantly coming to Him to tell Him we are bad off. We must seem to be unaware." (*Cons. et souv.*, p. 58) Who doesn't let any occasion to make a little sacrifice slip by, and this at the age of eleven?

Is it so easy to dream of a monastery where one is unknown, where one will have to undergo "exile of the heart"? "I dream of a monastery where I would be unknown, where I would have to suffer poverty, lack of affection, in short, exile of the heart." (Ms C, folio 10)

Thérèse must have seen that around her, her fervor was not very commonplace: "Oh, how few perfect religious, who do nothing any old way and lackadaisically, saying to themselves, I am not bound to do this, after all . . . There is no great harm to speak here, to satisfy myself in that . . . How rare those sisters who do everything as well as possible! Yet these are the happiest. Thus as regards silence, how good for the soul, what failings against charity and how much suffering of all kinds it prevents. I speak especially of silence because here is where are the most failings." (CJ, Aug. 6)

She herself struck those around her by the quality of her silence and her ponderation in everything. Here as elsewhere though, no one is perfect just because he'd like to be.

Yes, this is inimitable, at first writing anyway, or more exactly it is beyond the powers of nature. Thérèse was well aware of this, she who felt so poor, so small in everything, so weak, and who at the same time saw herself so flooded with graces that she dared write that she could not imagine a soul more heaped with graces than hers. Her fiery love is then first of all the work of grace, which is what is to be admired in Thérèse than Thérèse herself.

"What beauty? . . . I do not see my beauty at all. I see only the graces I have received from the good Lord . . ." (CJ, Aug. 10)

What then are those of us who are poor to do if grace does not come? God is master of His gifts and we cannot constrain Him to favor us. This is what those who do not much buy her doctrine blame in it: a protected childhood, parents living for God alone, four sisters who all wind up entering the convent. Even those gifts of nature joined to those of grace: intelligence, considerateness, a sensitive conscience, physical charm; these all make up a hardly ordinary assemblage.

This is a bit touching up the picture, in which our times would rather tend to root out the more human elements, but even if Thérèse had walked on nothing but roses, even if she was able to cry out in a burst of gratitude that it seemed to her impossible that a soul might be more loved by God than hers, it must not be forgotten that she added she was *sure* that Love could be still more lavish to someone providing . . .

This is where the door will stand wide open for us.

Only now do we come to her appeal for all. Thérèse's holiness is not abundance of natural and supernatural gifts, it is not her desires. She explained this very well to Sister Marie du Sacré-Coeur after she had sent her what would become Manuscript B: "How can you ask me if it is possible for you to love God as I have? . . . Had you understood the story of my little bird, you would not ask me that question. My desires for martyrdom *are nothing*, these are not what give me the limitless trust I feel in my heart. To tell the truth, it is spiritual riches which make us unjust, when we complacently rest upon them believing they are something great . . . These desires are a consolation Jesus sometimes grants to weak souls like mine (these souls are numerous), but when He does not give this consolation, it is a privilege grace. Recall these words of Father (*Footnote:* Father Pichon, in a retreat): 'The martyrs suffered joyfully, the King of martyrs suffered in sorrow.' Yes, Jesus said,

'Father, take away this chalice from me.' Darling Sister, how can you say after that that my desires are the mark of my love? . . . How I feel that this is not at all what pleased in my little soul. What pleases Him *is seeing my smallness and my poverty, the blind hope I have in His mercy* . . . This is my only treasure, darling Godmother. Why should not this treasure be yours?" (LT, Sept. 17, 1896)

Thérèse's sanctity is "a disposition of the heart which makes us humble and small in the arms of God, aware of our weakness and confident to the point of boldness in the goodness of the Father." This text, which in the most recent studies on Thérèse has been found not to be directly hers, nonetheless truly agrees with everything she otherwise says on the problem and is very well stated. Yet, since we are in a period of history when authenticity is well regarded, here is another, which is both from Thérèse and right for us all. In the bargain, it perfectly includes her double thrust of loving Jesus and of making Him loved.

"Oh, Jesus, if only I could tell all little souls how ineffable is Your condescendence! . . . I sense that if You did the impossible and found a soul weaker, smaller than mine, You would be pleased to heap it with still greater favors, *if it abandoned itself with complete trust to Your infinite mercy*. Why though, O Jesus, desire to communicate Your secrets of love? Are not You alone the One Who taught me them, and can You not reveal them to others?" (Ms B, folio 5)

We must beg Thérèse to communicate to us this secret, to reveal it to souls which have not yet discovered it, who dare not truly believe in it, who dare not commit their whole lives upon this way of trust and love, yet which they thirst for. What must be done to achieve this?

To me He gave His mercy:

Thérèse's trust, which is genuine theological hope, cannot be viewed apart from God's infinite *Mercy*, of which she had a very particular sense. She was conscious too of the grace this intuition represented.

"It seems to me that if all creatures had the same graces I have, the good Lord would be feared by no one, but madly loved. Not shaking but out of love no soul would consent to causing Him sorrow . . . I understand that all souls cannot be alike, there must be different families in order to honor especially each one of God's perfections. To me He has given His infinite Mercy, through which I contemplate and adore the other divine perfections! They all appear to me then radiating with love, even justice (perhaps still more than the others) seems clothed in love." (Ms A, folio 83)

Thérèse herself pointed out that she had

67

clearly explained herself on the relations between justice and the Lord's mercy in a letter to Father Roulland. Here are its main passages: "I know one must be very pure to appear before the God of all holiness, but I also know that the Lord is infinitely just. This justice, which frightens so many souls, is the subject of my joy and trust. Being just is not only exercising severity in punishing the guilty, but also recognizing right intentions and rewarding virtues. I hope as much from God's justice as from His mercy. It is because He is just that He 'is compassionate and filled with meekness, slow to punish and abounding in mercy.' For He knows our frailness. He remembers that we are but dust. As a father is tender for his children, so the Lord has compassion for us! . . . That, Brother, is what I think of God's justice. My way is all trust and love. I do not understand souls who are afraid of so kind a friend . . . A single word (of Holy Scripture) discloses to my soul infinite horizons, perfection seems to me easy: I see that it suffices to recognize one's nothingness and to abandon one's self like a child in the arms of the good Lord." (LT, May 9, 1897)

Abbé Bellière, of course, had his share of confidence as well, being so much in need of it: "Since it has been given to me also to understand the love of the heart of Jesus, I confess it has banned from my heart all fear! The memory of my faults humiliates me, leads me never to lean on my strength, which is only weakness, but this memory speaks still more of mercy and love. When with a completely filial trust one casts one's faults in the brazier of Love, how can they not be devoured irretrievably?" (LT, June 21, 1897)

"You love Saint Augustine and Saint Magdalen, those souls to whom 'many sins have been remitted because they have loved much.' So do I love them, I love their repentance and above all . . . their loving boldness . . . I sense that her (Magdalen's) heart understood the abysses of love and mercy of the Heart of Jesus, and that however sinful she was, that heart of love is not only disposed to forgive her, but also to lavish on her the benefits of His divine intimacy, to raise her to the highest summits of contemplation." (*ibid.*)

"For those who love Him and who, after each inconsiderateness cast themselves in His arms asking Him pardon, Jesus quivers with joy. He tells His angels what the father of the prodigal son said to his servants, 'Don him with his first robe, place a ring on his finger and rejoice.' Oh, Brother! How little known are Jesus' goodness and merciful love! . . . It is true that to enjoy these treasures we must humble ourselves and recognize our nothingness, and that is what many souls do not want to do, but, my little Brother, this is not the way you behave, so

the way of simple and loving trust suits you well
. . ." (LT, July 26, 1897)

Here we cannot help thinking of Thérèse's
calm assurance concerning purgatory. Here she
was only being logical, but also quite ahead of her
time. In fact, what would one ever do going to
purgatory if one believed that "when one casts
one's faults with such filial trust in the devouring
brazier of Love," they are "irretrievably con-
sumed"? Provided of course one believes in the
devouring power of Love.

Sister Fébronie, who defended the rights of
divine justice, got her earful on the problem!
Thérèse, yet so mild in common life, does not
hesitate to tell her, "Sister, you want God's justice,
you shall have God's justice! A soul receives exactly
what it expects from God." (François de Ste-Marie,
vol. II, p. 61)

To another:

"Sister Marie-Philomène, you are not trusting
enough, you are too afraid of the good Lord. I
assure you this afflicts Him. Do not fear purgatory
on account of the pain you suffer there, but desire
not to go there in order to please God Who im-
poses this expiation so regretfully. As long as you
seek to please Him in all things, if you trust unwav-
eringly that He purifies you each instant in His
love, leaving in you no trace of sin, be quite sure

you shall not go to purgatory." (Obituary circular letter of Sr. M.-Phil.)

For herself of course she had no fear whatsoever. It was quite the opposite of presumption. Yet, the considerateness of her love could not bear even to hear those she loved consider an eventual stay in that place in which Saint Catherine of Genoa is nevertheless said to have stated that one is nowheres better off except in paradise. (It is true that she also said one was nowheres worse off except in hell.)

"When we would speak to her of purgatory, for us she would say, 'Oh, how you grieve me! You greatly insult God in believing you will go to purgatory. For one who loves there can be no purgatory.' " (Letter of Sr. M. de l'Euch. to M. Guérin, July 8, 1897)

This is likewise the place to speak of her act of offering to merciful Love. Again something to be rightly understood.

This business of victim, of offering, of holocaust, etc. frightens certain souls. Yet here again is a little invention from Thérèse's heart always eager to give the Lord her best, most purely. Now, once well aware of one's poverty and weakness, what more can one give than to be the most widely open possible to receive continually a mercy which asks only to fill our wretchedness?

71

"In the evening of this life, I shall appear before You with empty hands, for I ask you not, Lord, to count my works. All our just works are spotted in Your eyes. I want then to clothe myself in Your own justice and receive from Your Love eternal possession of Yourself . . . To live in an act of perfect love, I offer myself as a holocaust victim to Your merciful Love, begging You to consume me continually, letting the waves of infinite tenderness enclosed in You overflow in my soul so that I may become a martyr of Your Love, O my God! . . ."

"May this martyrdom, after having prepared me to appear before You, make me at last die, and may my soul throw itself forward without delay into the eternal embrace of Your merciful love. O my Beloved, with each beat of my heart I want to renew this offering an infinite number of times until, the shadows vanished, I might repeat to You my love in an endless face to face."

This is exactly the opposite of fear. The fruits of this openness to love, of this total abandonment, were not long in being felt: "Ah! Since that happy day it seems to me Love penetrates and surrounds me. Each instant this merciful Love seems to renew me and purify my soul, leaving in it no trace of sin . . . thus I cannot fear purgatory . . ." (Ms A, folio 84)

That "each instant" will never be over-exploited. Yet, at first reading is it even noticed? It is such a wonder. No faulty payments in the realm of love, everything is always new, continually purified, entirely held in the springing of life and pardon which the Lord generously infuses in us as we continue to love and as we return to our Source, Himself.

Even if she had on her conscience all the sins that can be committed, nothing would stop Thérèse. "With a heart broken with repentance," she would go cast herself into the arms of Jesus, knowing "how much He cherishes the prodigal child who comes back to Him." (Ms C, folio 36)

The poorer you will be:

You still have to know you are a prodigal and accept it!

For there is one condition for the discovery of God's infinite mercy and for the trust, also infinite, which it brings about. That condition is the *awareness of our misery and its acceptance.*

"Oh, Brother! How little Jesus' goodness and merciful love are understood! . . . True, to enjoy these treasures we must humble ourselves, recognize our nothingness, and this is what many souls do not want to do." (LT to Abbé Bellière, July 26, 1897, already quoted)

To her godmother, Sister Marie du Sacré-Coeur, who felt so sorry she did not come up to her little sister's ankle when what became Manuscript

B was addressed to her, Thérèse replied that nothing she wrote was inaccessible and that anyway that was not what made her most pleasing to the Lord: "What pleases Him is to see me love my smallness and my poverty, the blind hope I have in His mercy . . ."

"The weaker one is, without desires or virtues, the fitter one is for the operations of that consuming and transforming Love. The sole desire to be a victim suffices, but one must consent to remain always poor and without strength, and that is what is hard, for 'where find the truly poor in spirit' " (LT, Sept. 17, 1896, already quoted)

To Céline, Christmas, 1896:

"Fear not, the poorer you are, the more Jesus will love you."

To Father Roulland, May 9, 1897:

"I rejoice to be small, since only children and those who resemble them will be admitted to the heavenly banquet."

On July 6, 1893, at the age of twenty, she had already explained to Céline her helplessness and her trust, and her awareness of doing nothing by herself: "Directors have us advance in perfection by having us perform a great number of acts of virtue, and they are right, but my Director, who is Jesus, does not teach me to count my acts, He instructs me to do everything out of love, to refuse Him nothing, to be satisfied when He provides me the occasion to prove that I love Him, but this is done in peace and abandonment. Jesus does everything and I do nothing."

The essential is stated in what is most concise, when she encourages Céline, "The poorer you are, the more Jesus will love you."

Does not this movement of the heart of God echo as it were in our own heart when we spontaneously go towards those who suffer the most, towards the most disinherited? Thus was Saint Dominic, who had "a special grace of compassion for the poor and the afflicted, whose woes he bore in the inner sanctuary of his heart," or Bernanos, with his "craze for lost causes." The heart of God is of this nature, but in the superlative, to infinity. He is pleased to fill the humble: the Blessed Virgin sang it more than anyone in her Magnificat, but we don't believe it enough. Otherwise, would there be so much sadness over one's self, so much difficulty in accepting wretchedness and distress, so many inferiority complexes? Some of Saint Benedict's degrees of humility could here be recalled:

To acknowledge one's wretchedness in one's self.

To say so openly.

To accept that others say so.

Oh, no! All this is not pleasing to nature! Especially the last degree. Yet, what would one not accept to be loved by someone who loves? Now the poorer we are, the more Jesus will love us. So? We have to be a little logical!

"One feels such great peace in being absolutely poor, in counting solely on the good Lord," Thérèse wrote this to Mother Agnès, August 6, 1897, in the following context: "I can rely on nothing, on none of my works, to have confidence. Thus, I would have so wanted to be able to say to myself: I have paid all my debts to the dead. This poverty though was for me a true light, a true grace. I thought that I had never in my life paid a single one of my debts to God, that this was for me true riches and power, if I wanted . . . I remembered with great sweetness these words in the canticle of Saint John of the Cross: 'Pay all debts.' I had always applied this to Love . . . I sense that this grace cannot be rendered . . ." (CJ, Aug. 6)

All this was fed directly from the gospel, from Jesus' keyword on his "character," made of meekness and humility, from the One Who was God made man: "I no longer find anything in books, except in the gospel. That book is enough for me. I listen with delight to these words of Jesus: 'Learn from me that I am meek and humble of heart.' Then I have peace according to His sweet promise: 'And you shall find rest for your little souls.' " (CJ, May 15)

This peace is beyond criticisms, but also

beyond praises: "All creatures can pore over her, admire her, weigh her down with their praises, I don't know why, but this could not add a single drop of false joy to the genuine joy she savors in her heart in seeing what she is in the eyes of God: a poor little nothing, nothing more." (Ms C, folio 2) "She has long ago understood that God needs no one (still less herself than others) to do good on earth." (Ms C, folio 3) "You may have remembered that the Lord is often pleased to grant wisdom to the little ones and that one day, transported with joy, He blessed His Father for having hidden His secrets from the prudent and for having revealed them to the littlest." (Ms C, folio 4)

Words of Jesus which, each time we hear them, should transport us with joy, and with the desire to know those secrets of the Father, by being, like His Son, meek and humble.

We only need to love Him:

To summarize, if it is clear that love is the center of Thérèse's life and doctrine, it is no less clear that for her the road which leads to the fullness of love is that of absolute trust in the infinite mercy of God, and that it is impossible to know the meaning of divine mercy without at the same time accepting its radical poverty. In this way, trust and abandonment, amounting to two synonyms, is the most expansive and the simplest way there is. They flood away our very faults. According to Thérèse, a single fault is to be feared, lack of trust: "What offends Jesus, what wounds His heart is lack of trust."

Thérèse had already written this to Marie Guérin on May 30, 1889, when she was sixteen. She was not to change with the years.

Céline was to receive the same confidences and the same advice in 1893: "O, Céline! How easy it is to please Jesus, to ravish His heart! We only have to love him, without looking at ourselves, without examining our defects too much . . . Your Thérèse is not on the heights at this moment, but Jesus teaches her to profit from everything, from the good and from the evil she finds in herself . . . He teaches her to play at the bank of love, or rather no, He plays for her, without telling her how He goes about it, for that is His business, and not Thérèse's. Her concern is to abandon herself, to give herself up without reserving anything, not even to enjoy knowing how much the bank pays." (LT, July 6, 1893)

Are we to miss such a chance as this: not to look at our defects too much? For Thérèse's sanctity does not consist in imitating the works of great saints—as used to be read in the common of martyrs: what good is it to admire the works of the saints if not to imitate them! She had first of all to believe that God is the One Who does everything, and to accept being radically poor.

"Even had I accomplished all the works of Saint Paul, I would still deem myself 'a useless servant,' but this is exactly what constitutes my joy, for, having nothing, I shall receive everything from God." (CJ, June 23)

"I am very glad I shall soon go to heaven, but I think of these words of God, 'I carry my reward with me to render to each according to his works,' I tell myself that in my case He will be quite embarrassed. I have no works! He will then be unable to render to me 'according to my works.' Well, He will then render to me according to His own works!" (CJ, May 15)

Les mains vides (Empty Hands) is the title of a small book which in three words condenses a masterful study on trust in Thérèse. In it is said there was at first a very strong fear of offending God. This fear "would little by little give way to a limitless trust in His mercy . . . Thérèse would have to discover mercy as the center of her own life, that mercy is there for the little one, that it is for him because he is little, and how great it is for whoever receives it as a little one and trusts in it . . . The multi-valued symbol of littleness instead of being mainly humility would henceforth be mainly trust." (*Footnote: Les mains vides*, by Conrad de Meester.)

Once more, we must believe all the way that God runs everything with an infinite love, and cannot deceive "those who run along the way of love." Profoundly deceive, for of course outwardly there can be winds which are against us, but deep down, "All is grace," and "Lord, You fill me with joy by everything You do," two of Thérèse's major statements we shall come back to.

Is there not a way of apprehending events and people which in the end is nothing but fear of God, and not filial fear? Thérèse affirms on the contrary: "We who run along the way of love, I find, must not think of anything painful that can happen to us in the future, for that is lacking in trust, and is like meddling in creating." (CJ, July 23)

Meddling in creating! Inventing the future in the imagination so as to anticipate Providence by apprehending It and thus denying It. Yet, we are called to create after a fashion, but not *ex nihilo*, not on fantasies of the mind either. How distinguish true prudence and foresight from wrong uneasiness? Generally, when uneasiness is not according to God, it shuts off energy, prevents advancing, living. If normal care and prudent wisdom prevail though, the climate of trust lived in creates a new dynamism in which genuine humility has all its room.

"Those who hope in the Lord
renew their strength,

wings come to them like eagles'
they run without weariness,
they walk without fatigue."

(Is 40:31)

Since love of neighbor is all one with love of God, something else must be added. To enter into God's intimacy if one is paralyzed with fear is difficult. Likewise, it will not be easy to penetrate into the heart of one's neighbor if he is approached with distrust, or at least without enough trust. The same movement of trust which must open us to the fullness of the love of God will also open us to the fullness of the love of one's neighbor.

Whereas if we approach others with a distrustful reserve, it will be difficult to understand them fully. Something will then always escape us.

In his book on brotherly love in Saint Thérèse of the Child Jesus, Father Descouvemont saw in pride the greatest obstacle to brotherly encounter. One might wonder if it is not rather a lack of trust. Yet, after all it is the same, for when one gives in to a lack of trust in God or in one's neighbor, it is because one shuts one's self within one's own judgment, often so limited, and because one then is wrong and proud enough to believe this the norm of everything. This is the opposite of true charity, which believes all, hopes all, bears all, and thinks no evil. (1 Cor 13: 4-7)

What grace is lost when trust is missed! But it

is always time to enter. All our past doubts, all our faults are "like a drop of water thrown into an ardent brazier." (CJ, July 11) From now on anybody, everybody can offer God all his incapableness and stubbornly await for help with complete trust.

"I for my part consider myself as a weak little bird covered only with a light down. I am not an eagle, I have only its eyes and heart, for in spite of my extreme smallness I dare gaze upon the divine Sun, the Sun of Love, and my heart feels within itself all the aspirations of the Eagle . . ." (Ms B, folio 4)

Nothing can ever discourage this weakling, "neither wind, nor rain, and if dark clouds eventually hide the Star of Love, the little bird will not move, it knows that beyond the clouds its Sun is always shining, that its brightness cannot for an instant be eclipsed." (Ms B, folio 5)

A limitless trust sustained her attitude: "O Jesus, let me in my excess of gratitude, let me tell You that Your Love reaches to the point of folly . . . Faced with such folly, how can You expect my heart not to leap forward towards You?" (*ibid.*)

This trust is within our reach. Thérèse said so. All that is needed is to be little and poor and to look away from all judgment, both of men and of God, for, "The little ones shall be judged with extreme mildness. We can remain little even in the most formidable offices, even living very long. Had I died at the age of eighty years old, and had been in China, everywhere, I would have died, I know it, just as small as I am today. It is written that in the end the Lord shall rise up to save all the meek and the humble of the earth. It does not say judge, but save." (CJ, Sept. 25)

4

What He Does Is What I Like

Jacques Maritain said that the little way of Thérèse is the "way of poor people," but he adds: "It is a way which requires great courage. Abandonment to the Loved One takes over everything, gets through all the stages Jesus will have us go through—it is up to Him to know, and will lead wherever Jesus wants, in the light or night." (*Footnote: Le Paysan de la Garonne*, p. 339)

* Yes, this way does require great courage. We must not be misled: Saint Thérèse of Lisieux's meekness covers over a very great strength; her way of trust is a constant self-denial. Much self-surrender is needed for abandonment, even though it be into the hands of God. Much will-power is needed too. No doubt this is where Thérèse's message has been most deformed by making of her little way an easy way. If it is a way which is

accessible to all by that kind of clever invention of trust as the road of love, it does not provide us with a cheap sanctity, for cheap sanctity does not exist. Céline testified at her sister's trial that the saint's dominant virtue was fortitude. That is right. Attention needs only to be drawn to this point for "little" Thérèse's fortitude to show through everywhere. In fact, the grace of her conversion at Christmas was a grace of fortitude. "Little Thérèse had found again the strength of soul she had lost at the age of four and a half and she would forever keep it!" (Ms A, folio 45)

Until then she cried excessively. When Marie entered Carmel, she broke down: "Each time I went by the door of her room, I knocked until she opened the door for me and I embraced her with all my heart. I wanted to store up kisses for all the time I was to be deprived of them . . ." (Ms A, folio 43)

At that time, "she was hurt by everything," and when she began to console herself for what she had cried for, she "cried for having cried." (Ms A, folio 44)

Christmas Eve "Jesus, the sweet little child of one hour, changed the night of my soul into torrents of light . . . On this night when He became weak and suffering for love of me, He made me strong and courageous, He clothed me with His armor, and since that blessed night in no battle have I been defeated, but on the contrary I marched from victory to victory and commenced so to speak a course of a giant . . ." (*ibid.*)

From then on Thérèse enjoyed "the grace of being dejected by no passing event." (Ms A, folio 43) She showed it!

She was intrepid, the very opposite of "human prudence trembling at each step, daring not, so to speak, to set her foot down." (Ms A, folio 75) Twice she quotes a passage from the *Imitation* which she knew by heart, "Never does Love find anything impossible because it believes everything is possible and everything is allowed it." (Notice by the way the sole source of her fortitude is Love. We are still following the same line of thought.) To love while wanting to control everything and ultimately to possess everything, to give one's self but without losing too much is to love poorly. The love Thérèse speaks of is bold and fears nothing, which made her go very far! Not the least quietism in her abandonment, nor the least fear either. Here must be recalled the resolution on the day of her first communion, "I will not be discouraged." (Quoted by Fr. François de Ste-Marie, Manuscripts, vol. II p. 27) This already amounted to saying, I shall never lose confidence, but a confidence perceived from the angle of fortitude, and even of effort.

"Many souls say, I do not have the strength to accomplish a certain sacrifice. Let them do what I did, make a great effort. God never refuses that first grace which gives the courage to act. After that the heart is strengthened and one goes from victory to victory." (CJ, Aug. 8)

"If we are struggling with a disagreeable soul, we must not be disheartened, we must never leave it. Let us always have in our mouth the "sword of the spirit" to correct its wrongs. We must not let things go to keep our rest. We must always do battle even without hope of winning the battle. What does success matter? What God asks of us is not to stop from the fatigue of the struggle, not to become discouraged . . . We must do our duty to the end." (CJ, April 6)

"If I am not loved, so much the worse! I myself tell the whole truth: let those who don't want to know it not come to me." (CJ, April 18)

Much unity in all this, which does not contradict but rather balances off the deep awareness Thérèse had of her helplessness and weakness.

* Yes, Thérèse herself showed at length how weak she felt, with, in spite of all, a background of Norman robustness and a bit of stubbornness. This has been so sufficiently written about that it is unnecessary to go into detail. What needs to be shown here is that Thérèse's fortitude is not a matter of sensitiveness or of natural impulse, but only of her will, the will as the profound orientation of her being, as the faculty of loving. What proves this is her *attitude in the face of suffering*, that touchstone of true love, of true fortitude.

Father Gaucher has written a whole book on the "passion" of Thérèse, but it concerns only the sufferings, enormous, of her last months and of her last sickness. Now Thérèse loved in suffering all her life.

"That little glass is the image of my life," she said some months before dying, showing a medicine which looked like gooseberry liqueur.

"Yesterday Sister Thérèse de Saint-Augustin said to me, 'I hope you are drinking a good liqueur!' I answered her, O Sister de St-Augustin, 'It is the worst thing I drink!' Well, dear little Mother, that is what appeared to the eyes of creatures. It has always seemed to them that I was drinking exquisite liqueurs, but it was bitterness. I say bitterness but no! For my life has not been bitter, because I was able to make my joy and my sweetness out of all bitterness." (CJ, July 30)

This last sentence must not be forgotten, without which reality would be deformed, for what is beautiful is not that there was so very much suffering, but that everything was turned into love. That is what Thérèse wanted to be known:

"I found happiness and joy on earth, but solely in suffering, for I have suffered much here below. This should be made known to souls . . . I had a continuous desire to suffer, since my first communion, since I had asked Jesus to change into bitterness for me all the consolations of the earth. I did not think however to make them my joy. This grace was granted me only later. Until then it was like a spark hidden in the ashes, like the blossoms of a tree, which in time are to become fruit. Always seeing the flowers fall though, that is, letting myself go into tears when I suffered, I said to myself with shock and sadness: it then will never be anything but desires." (CJ, July 31)

Inefficacious desires, such as everybody has so many of, desires whose authenticity remains unproved by any deeds. Now love in Thérèse did not remain at this stage. By fully accepting the whole of the trials allotted her, she affirmed and proved her love of God: heartbreaks of all kinds, physical suffering, and that long night of faith, which for months was her greatest cross, until her death.

"It is very easy to write nice things on suffering, but to write is nothing, nothing! One has to be in it to know." Here, however, she was not backing down, for she immediately stated: "I now sense clearly that what I have said and written is true for everything . . . It is true that I wanted to suffer greatly for God and it is true I still desire to." (CJ, Sept. 25)

She was asked if it was not too hard to suffer so much.

"No, that still allows me to tell God that I love Him, I find that is sufficient." (CJ, July 30)

The prospect of death, for which, it must be recognized, she was ready, was almost continually spoken of with the sick patient. This may understandably seem strange and even unwholesome, but for Thérèse all this context had long ago been simply related to the Cross of Jesus. Her longing for suffering was nowise morbid and was well associated with much joy and humor. What gave her the strength to suffer so, to like and even to desire suffering was love of God and of neighbor. Nothing else. To love Jesus and to prove it by following Him on the road He Himself had traced. To make Him loved by accepting and offering up all the sufferings, small and great, which came.

"Never would I have believed it was possible to suffer so much! Never! Never! I can only explain it by the ardent desires I had to save souls." (CJ, Sept. 30)

She furthermore explained this clearly in many places: "When one wants to attain a goal, one must take the means. Jesus made me understand that it was by the Cross that He wanted to give me souls. My longing for suffering grew as suffering increased." (Ms A, folio 69)

"These words of Isaiah, 'Who has believed your word . . . He is without splendor, without beauty, etc. . .' became the whole foundation of my devotion to the Holy Face, or rather, the foundation of all my piety. I too desired to be without beauty, alone to tread the wine in the wine press, unknown by any creature." (CJ, Aug. 5)

"I am thinking of the words of Saint Ignatius of Antioch. I too must by suffering be crushed to become the flour of God." (CJ, Aug. 10)

This is something that goes away back, since around the time when her older sister Marie had carefully prepared her for her first communion. As we know, she heard herself told that she would not walk along the way of suffering, "but that the good Lord would always carry her as a child." (Ms A, folio 36) The little girl had ruminated this over and "The next day, after my communion, Marie's words came back to my mind. I felt the birth in my heart of a great desire for suffering and at the same time the intimate assurance that Jesus reserved for me a great number of crosses." This did not frighten her. "I felt flooded with consolations so great that I consider them as one of the greatest graces of my life. Suffering became my longing, it had charms which ravished me without knowing them well. Until then, I had suffered without loving suffering. Since that day I felt a genuine love for it. I also felt the desire of loving only God, of finding joy only in Him." (ibid.)

There in that last sentence is the key: to desire to suffer (a desire really not in style today, and which cannot be natural at any time!) is for Thérèse to desire to love.

Later, when her entrance into Carmel is right near, this desire's orientation became more precise, its motive more conscious: "I desire only one thing when I shall be in Carmel, always to suffer for Jesus. Life passes by so fast that really it is better to have a very beautiful crown and a little suffering than to have an ordinary one without suffering. For a pain endured with joy, when I think that during all eternity one will love God better! Then, by suffering souls can be saved. Oh, Pauline, if at the hour of my death I could have a soul to offer Jesus, how happy I would be! There would be a soul snatched from the fire of hell and who would bless God for eternity." (LT, March, 1888)

It is not a matter of suffering just to suffer, but to suffer in order to love more, and to make loved! It was very early that Thérèse understood that *it is not those who say Lord, Lord, who will enter into the Kingdom of heaven*. The love which is the center of her life must be proved, coined, and since God Himself has proved to us His love on the Cross, there is no other way. You can say or do what you like to get out of it, but you can't! It is like *English without Effort* or *Calculus with a Smile*, and all the recipes for success without effort. Paradise without pain would be just too nice! Thérèse has given us the example of a genuine love, of a love which acquired the fullness of its being, and which expressed itself by welcoming all suffering, with a valiantness and a conviction which held up until the last moment, to the extreme limit of her energy. Was she not still groaning, just before her death, on the threshold of her entrance "into life":

"Oh, I would not want to suffer for any less time." (CJ, Sept. 30)

It must be well understood, if we truly wish to follow Thérèse, that her way of trust will not dispense us from trying hard. This is impossible, but she will make us sure that God will give us the strength to try hard and to get ourselves out of our ruts, that He Himself in the end will give us the strength to suffer for His love and in loving Him, to welcome all suffering out of love, in union with Jesus in His Agony or on the Cross. This is the way we must go, willingly or unwillingly. For Thérèse of course it was "willingly" and with good will. This is her surest means of apostolate.

When the correspondence with Abbé Bellière was entrusted to her with the aim of helping this tormented young seminarian, that "sweet mission" would be fulfilled in her eyes only by prayer and suffering far more than by letters: "I sense that the surest means of attaining my goal is to pray and suffer." (LT, Dec. 26, 1896)

"Let us not believe we can love without suffering, without suffering very much," she had already written to Céline on April 26, 1889. To Mother Agnès, July 8, 1897: "It is by prayer and sacrifice only that we can be useful to the Church." (CJ, July 8)

This comes down to nothing else but walking in the footsteps of Christ the Redeemer. Many souls of good will intensely desire the fullness of love, and, apparently, do not succeed. God alone can judge the reality of these failures. Nevertheless, one can imagine that a great desire to love genuinely can often be found to coexist with a kind of inability to accept suffering, self-denial and, ultimately, with a certain lack of will power, of the will as the faculty of loving, the power to love in truly losing one's self, of loving by giving one's self. Or the strength to persevere. What is lacking is not good will but simply will.

"Unfortunate man that I am," (Rm 7:24) Saint Paul had already exclaimed, *"the good I will I do not, and the evil I will not I fall into!"* (Rm 7:15)

Now just so current a flaw must not discourage us. Thérèse too was very weak, nor did she overcome just by sheer strength, nor by a placid abandonment, which would be nothing but giving up, but by trust and love, according to the reasoning we have seen: "God could not inspire unrealizable desires." (Ms C, folio 2)

* No, if Thérèse was not left to her own resources, neither did she exercise in loving in a garden of roses.

"It is most important for the soul to exercise a great deal in Love so that using itself up rapidly, it may hardly stop here below but may promptly succeed in seeing its God face to face." (CJ, July 27) How did she live these words of Saint John of the Cross which she enthusiastically repeated to herself around the age of seventeen? Where did she draw the strength from, for this continual "exercise" of love?

There is no getting out of this "vicious" circle. If Thérèse's strength and fortitude allowed her to persevere in love through all the suffering of body and soul, love in her was the source of strength, a love submissive in all things to the will of God, far more, embracing it; far more yet, running ahead to greet it and embrace it sooner and harder. More than submission, it was an *accord of the will to God's will*, an accord which was more and more without constraint, until the perfect harmony of the final months.

Too often God's will is seen as something imposed upon us from without, something to constrain us and which is apprehended, which is often sought for with a certain anguish, whereas we should think that for those who seek Him, God prepares the heart for what He wants to give. His will springs from within the soul itself. Is it not in this sense that it has been possible to speak of "inventing" the will of God, in the first meaning of "invenio," to come upon or find? Love has us find

God's will in ourselves and accords all our being to it. Thérèse understood this well. This is why her love gave out such a pure sound.

First her eyes were on God Whom she loved, and when someone is loved everything is accepted from him, even those sufferings of which he is or seems to be responsible, even his defects. God of course has no defects, but He may have views which from without seem opposed to ours. Thérèse gazed upon Him, and what He wanted became hers. By her very love she was accorded. She was truly impassioned for the will of God. Just as she stated that she could not be charitable if Jesus Himself did not love in her all her sisters, so too God's will passing through her became her strength and lifted up her will to it.

To live or to die then is of little importance to her! To suffer, again of little importance.

"Love seems to me able to make up for a long life. Jesus is not concerned about time, since there isn't anymore in heaven. He must be concerned only with love. Ask Him to give me also much. I do not ask for sensible love, but sensed only by Jesus. Oh, how sweet it is to love Him!" (LT to Mother Agnès, Sept. 3, 1890)

"I shall consent, if it is His will, to walk all my life along the dark road I follow provided I arrive one day at the end of the mountain of love, but I do not believe this will be here below." (*ibid.*, Sept. 1, 1890)

"My fiancé tells me nothing and I tell him nothing either except that I love Him more than myself. I feel in the bottom of my heart that this is true, for I am more His than my own." (*ibid.*, Aug. 30-31, 1890)

All the preceding Thérèse wrote at the age of seventeen, during her profession retreat. She had not yet arrived at the "end of the mountain of love," but was already terrifically well-oriented. The first step upon this road had been from her infancy, to work towards breaking her own will. How foolish and how time-wasting always to want to affirm one's will! Instead of being free, with the freedom of love, one is bound, imprisoned by that woeful will for independence, for self-determination, which is the opposite of genuine freedom in God. Yet Thérèse was not lacking in personality, as her mother testified in many letters, even when she was still but a spoiled little girl borne by everybody.

Later, before her entrance into Carmel, so around the age of fifteen: "My mortifications consisted in breaking my own will always ready to impose, to refrain from answering back, to render little services without showing them off, not leaning back when I was seated, etc. By practicing these trifles I was preparing myself to become Jesus' fiancée." (Ms A, folio 68)

"God did not want me as a plain soldier. I was immediately armed as a knight and I left for war against myself in the spiritual realm, by self-denial and small, hidden sacrifices. I found peace and humility in this obscure combat where nature has no hold." (NV, Aug. 3)

This is important, but once more, this "obscure combat" is not led by sheer strength. In Thérèse it is always accompanied by meekness, trust, acceptance of her helplessness. The more her life advanced the more it gave the impression that her step was as in step with God. Between her soul and her God, a kind of continual accord resulted in an inalterable peace. If already on the day of her first communion she was able to speak of a "fusion" between Jesus and herself, nevertheless there indeed seems to have been a truly "giant's course" between that sensible grace of childhood and the profoundness of fusion in her will which marked her last months and which was expressed all through her sickness, through her almost continuous physical and spiritual sufferings. What God wanted became completely her own will, and as her heart was accorded beforehand to the will of God, she who accepted no making believe and was hardly given to empty words, could exclaim in all truth:

"Lord, *You fill me with joy by everything You do.*

For is there any joy greater than to suffer for Your love?" (Ms C, folio 7)

How can the importance of this profound attitude be put across, how can this identity of will with God's, which gives so much strength to advance in trust, but which also starts from trust—how can it be made desirable? Thérèse will explain it to us by the itinerary she herself followed: before there is this accord of wills which gives so much freedom and joy, the will of God must first be espoused in our own will, and, of course, this is no matter of sentiment. This wedding can be accomplished only in confidence, an absolute confidence that what God wants is best for us and for all.

First we must try. "Often God wants only our will. He requires all, and if we refuse Him the least thing, He loves us too much to give in to us, but as soon as our will conforms to His, then He acts with us the way He acted in the old days with Abraham." (LT to Céline, July 18, 1894)

Who has not experienced this in the little daily battles of the imperfect soul? Who has not finally seen that "the sole happiness is always to try to find the portion Jesus gives us to delight?" (LT to Léonie, July 17, 1897)

After this phase of effort, one day it is discovered that God causes what He wants to give us to be desired, that He hollows out the soul in order to fill it up, a kind of dissatisfaction, a desire for something more, whatever the price.

"Ah, the Lord is so good to me that it is impossible for me to fear Him. He has always made me desire what He wanted to give me. Thus shortly before my trial against faith, I reasoned this. Really I do not have any great exterior trials, and for any interior ones God would have to change my way. I do not believe He will, yet I cannot always live like this at rest . . . The answer was not long in coming and showed me that the One I love is not short of means." (Ms C, folio 31)

"Ah, like Jesus' own, I wanted my face to be truly hidden, that on earth no one might recognize me! I thirsted to suffer and to be forgotten . . . How merciful is the way by which God has always led me. Never has He made me desire something without giving me it, so too His bitter chalice seemed delightful to me." (Ms A, folio 71)

Of course what were Thérèse's desires have to be considered, always in the line of love.

"One day when I had particularly desired being humiliated, a novice happened to take it upon herself to satisfy me so well that I thought of Shimei cursing David. I said to myself: Yes, it is indeed the Lord who orders her to tell me all these things . . . My soul delightfully relished the bitter food which was so abundantly served ." (Ms C, folio 27)

An experience of this kind, both pure grace and the fruit of a long faithfulness, could not help logically generating an immense desire to do nothing for one's self, and for a greater abandonment.

Now the accord was effected without effort:

"I no more desire to die than to live, that is if I had to choose, I would like better to die, but since it is the good Lord Who chooses for me, I like better what He wants. *What He does is what I like.*" (CJ, May 27)

That is right. The signs were there in Thérèse, the fruits of the Holy Spirit, Who had completely taken possession of her whole being, those signs which were: joy, peace, brotherly love.

"What He does is what I like."

Which one of us would not desire to come to this, to lay down his soul in the hands of the Father at the moment of death, whatever its form, in that grand movement of abandonment and love which was Jesus' on the Cross? Who though does not also feel that, although it was normal for Jesus, the perfect Son, to be totally accorded with the Father, for an ordinary human being it is a very great grace. Now God alone can give that grace. How can it be obtained? What road must be taken?

Thérèse again has given the answer, her last word on the matter: ALL IS GRACE.

"No doubt it is a great grace to receive the

sacraments, but when God does not permit it, it is all right just the same." (CJ, June 5)

Because all is Love for whoever goes along with God, trusting completely in Him, trusting of course throughout all the circumstances of life, throughout all the instruments of Providence surrounding us, part of God's marvelous plan to bring back everything to its Source whence everything to Himself, Who is Love.

Conclusion

Thus, in Saint Thérèse of the Child Jesus, everything started from Love and everything was brought back to Love, love of God first of all.

This love of God was inseparable from the desire to make Him loved. Thérèse was profoundly an apostle in the best sense of the word, continually concerned with her neighbor, the closest: her family and her sisters in religion, and the farthest: missionaries out in space [sic: *missionnaires dans l'espace*] sinners in the order of grace. In her all this was one.

The characteristic mark of this love was trust, a trust which sprang forth at the meeting point of her poverty and God's mercy. It has been abundantly inventoried in learned papers. It is properly theological hope, offered to all.

For Thérèse it served as a spring-board to a more and more integral love, to the point of fusion of her will with God's. This is all love, for God is

Love, and His will is always a loving will.

What more can we desire?

We cannot desire this for ourselves alone, though. Such would be impossible and contrary to the nature of Love. Our love will be complete only if it leads after it all those around us, and beyond.

"Lord, I understand, when a soul has allowed itself to be captivated by the inebriating scent of Your perfumes, it could not run alone, all the souls it loves are led along after it. This is done without constraint, without effort, as a natural consequence of its attraction towards You. Just as a torrent casting itself impetuously into the ocean carries along after it everything it meets along its way, so too, O my Jesus, the soul which plunges into the shoreless ocean of Your love, draws with it all the treasures it possesses . . ." (Ms C, folio 34, already quoted)

Lines to fill the heart of a contemplative vocation with an immense joy. For in the life of faith it represents, as in that of every Christian no doubt, there is a boundless need to believe that "The more the fire of love enkindles my heart, the more I shall say, Draw me, the more to souls who approach me (poor useless little iron debris were I to go away from the divine brazier)—the more souls will run fast in the scent of the perfumes of their Beloved, for a soul kindled with love cannot remain inactive." (Ms C, folio 36)

A soul kindled with love cannot remain inactive!

Oh, there is a paradoxical criterion of the authenticity of contemplative life which provides us as with its touchstone. Contemplative life is the exact opposite of tranquillity and selfishness: it is the ec-stasy, the going out of self to plunge into the Beloved, to discover there all the secrets of His heart and to enlarge our own to the size of His.

"Seeming to give nothing, Magdalen (who remains at Jesus' feet listening to His sweet inflamed words) gives much more than Martha, tormented by many things and wanting her sister to imitate her. Jesus does not blame Martha's work . . . It is only the restlessness of His ardent hostess that He wanted to correct . . ." (Ms C, folio 36)

Restlessness: interior activism, which has us going in circles inside, and often outside, and stirring in vain, the opposite of trust and of love's true activity.

"All the saints understood this, more particularly those who filled the universe with the illumination of the evangelical doctrine. Is it not in prayer that Saints Paul, Augustine, John of the Cross, Thomas Aquinas, Francis, Dominic and so many other friends of God drew that knowledge of God which delights the greatest geniuses? A scholar has said, 'Give me a lever and a resting point and *I shall lift up the world.*' What Archimedes was unable to obtain because his request was not addressed to God and because it was made only from a material point of view, the saints obtained in all its fullness. The Almighty has given them for a resting point HIMSELF and HIM ALONE.

As a lever, prayer which inflames with a *fire of love*. This is how they lifted up the world. This is how the still militant saints lift it and how until the end of the world, the saints to come shall lift it too." (*ibid.*)

Thérèse was absolutely sure of what she advanced and she was right. Did she not prove it in lifting up the world herself, in a manner humanly unexplainable? The "fire of love" which inflames the saints was the one she felt burning in herself. *There was in my heart as a devouring fire enclosed in my bones. I exhausted myself to contain it, I could not bear it.* (Jr 20:9)

If each Christian thus lifted the world around him. . . . If each one fully believed in the strength of prayer, where Love dwells . . .

Thérèse has opened the road for us, here and now, wherever we are and whatever we do. We need only consent to suffer a little bit, yes, a little, for in the end love will always find it little, to hope much, for and against everything, and to love without measure.

"Love alone counts." (NV, Sept. 29)